Regents

SUCCESS STRATEGIES

High School English Language Arts (Common Core)

**Regents Test Review
for the New York
Regents Examinations**

Dear Future Exam Success Story:

Congratulations on your purchase of our study guide. Our goal in writing our study guide was to cover the content on the test, as well as provide insight into typical test taking mistakes and how to overcome them.

Standardized tests are a key component of being successful, which only increases the importance of doing well in the high-pressure high-stakes environment of test day. How well you do on this test will have a significant impact on your future, and we have the research and practical advice to help you execute on test day.

The product you're reading now is designed to exploit weaknesses in the test itself, and help you avoid the most common errors test takers frequently make.

How to use this study guide

We don't want to waste your time. Our study guide is fast-paced and fluff-free. We suggest going through it a number of times, as repetition is an important part of learning new information and concepts.

First, read through the study guide completely to get a feel for the content and organization. Read the general success strategies first, and then proceed to the content sections. Each tip has been carefully selected for its effectiveness.

Second, read through the study guide again, and take notes in the margins and highlight those sections where you may have a particular weakness.

Finally, bring the manual with you on test day and study it before the exam begins.

Your success is our success

We would be delighted to hear about your success. Send us an email and tell us your story. Thanks for your business and we wish you continued success.

Sincerely,

Mometrix Test Preparation Team

Need more help? Check out our flashcards at:
http://MometrixFlashcards.com/Regents

TABLE OF CONTENTS

Top 15 Test Taking Tips

1. Know the test directions, duration, topics, question types, how many questions
2. Setup a flexible study schedule at least 3-4 weeks before test day
3. Study during the time of day you are most alert, relaxed, and stress free
4. Maximize your learning style; visual learner use visual study aids, auditory learner use auditory study aids
5. Focus on your weakest knowledge base
6. Find a study partner to review with and help clarify questions
7. Practice, practice, practice
8. Get a good night's sleep; don't try to cram the night before the test
9. Eat a well balanced meal
10. Wear comfortable, loose fitting, layered clothing; prepare for it to be either cold or hot during the test
11. Eliminate the obviously wrong answer choices, then guess the first remaining choice
12. Pace yourself; don't rush, but keep working and move on if you get stuck
13. Maintain a positive attitude even if the test is going poorly
14. Keep your first answer unless you are positive it is wrong
15. Check your work, don't make a careless mistake

Reading

Literature

Explicit information

Explicit information includes facts and statements that are found directly in a passage or a story. It is not information that is hinted at or information you need to make a conclusion about. Explicit information may be found in many forms; it can be contained in a quote as well as in a description. It can be found in dialogue and in actions. This information can sometimes be used to support an inference. The answers to questions about explicit information are found through careful reading of the text. Attention is given to pertinent facts or other information. In fiction, details about characters, events, and setting can be both explicit and implicit.

Read the following excerpt and identify the information that is explicit.

> According to an ancient Greek legend, an inventor named Daedalus was imprisoned on an island by an angry king. His son, Icarus, was with him. The inventor came up with an escape plan. He created two pairs of wings from feathers and a wooden frame. He made one for himself and one for his son.

Explicit information is information found directly in the text. It is not inferred; it is not suggested. The explicit information in this excerpt is about the Greek myth that tells the story of the inventor Daedalus. The excerpt says that the inventor Daedalus and his son Icarus were imprisoned on an island by an angry king. It says that he had a plan of escape, and that he created two pairs of wings from feathers and a wooden frame. This information is found directly in the excerpt. It is not necessary to make any inferences or guesses to obtain this information.

Inference

An inference is a conclusion that a reader can make based on the facts and other information in a passage or a story. An inference is based both on what is found in a passage or a story and what is known from personal experience. For instance, a story may say that a character is frightened and that he can hear the sounds of wolves in the distance. Based on both what is in the text and personal knowledge, it might be a logical conclusion that the character is frightened because he hears the sound of wolves. A good inference is supported by the information in a passage. Inferences are different from explicit information, which is clearly stated in a passage. Inferences are not stated in a passage. A reader must put the information together to come up with a logical conclusion.

Read the excerpt and decide why Jana finally relaxed.

> Jana loved her job, but the work was very demanding. She had trouble relaxing. She called a friend, but she still thought about work. She ordered a pizza, but eating it did not help. Then her kitten jumped on her lap and began to purr. Jana leaned back and began to hum a little tune. She felt better.

You can draw the conclusion that Jana relaxes because her kitten jumped on her lap. The kitten purred, and Jana leaned back and hummed a tune. Then, she felt better. The excerpt does not explicitly say that this is the reason why she was able to relax. The text leaves the matter unclear. But, the reader can infer or make a "best guess" that this is the reason she is relaxing. This is a logical conclusion based on the information in the passage. It is the best conclusion a reader can make based on the information he or she has read. Inferences are based on the information in a passage, but they are not directly stated in the passage.

Determining the theme of a passage

The theme of a passage is what the reader learns from the text or the passage. It is the lesson or moral contained in the passage. A passage can have two or more themes that convey its overall idea. The theme or themes of a passage are often based on universal themes. They can frequently be expressed using well-known sayings about life, society, or human nature, such as "Hard work pays off" or "Good triumphs over evil." Themes are not usually stated explicitly. The reader must figure them out by carefully reading the passage. Themes are often the reason why passages are written; they give a passage unity and meaning. Themes are created through plot development. The events of a story help shape the themes of a passage.

Explain why "Take care of what you care about" accurately describes the theme of the following excerpt.

> Luca collected baseball cards. But, Luca wasn't very careful with them. He left them around the house. His dog liked to chew. Luca and his friend Bart were looking at his collection. Then, they went outside. When Luca got home, he saw his dog chewing on his cards. They were ruined.

This excerpt tells the story of a boy who is careless with his baseball cards and leaves them lying around. His dog ends up chewing them and ruining them. The lesson is that if you care about something, you need to take care of it. This is the point of the story. The theme is the lesson that a story teaches. Some stories have more than one theme, but this is not really true of this excerpt. The reader needs to figure out the theme based on what happens in the story. Sometimes, as in the case of fables, the theme is stated directly in the text. However, this is not usually the case.

Components of a story summary

A summary of a passage or a story should include the main ideas of a passage and also the important details that support the main ideas. It shouldn't just be a general statement about what a passage is about, but should include important events and other details that make the story what it is. In order to write an objective summary, you have to reflect on what the passage is about. A summary puts the information in a concise form. Consequently, summarizing is different from paraphrasing. Paraphrasing involves rewording the main idea and supporting ideas in a fairly detailed way; summarizing does not. Summaries afford the reader the opportunity to quickly review the main points of a passage and the important details.

Setting and characters

Without characters and setting, there is no story. They affect the plot of a story in many ways. The setting creates the background for the action. The setting could be someplace exotic or mundane, but wherever it is, it creates limitations for the characters. Characters are also essential to a story. They bring the story to life; it is their decisions, what they do, and how they act that creates the plot of a story and ultimately its theme. Characters can have good traits and bad traits. Analyzing what these are based on what a character does and says is an important aspect of comprehending the meaning of a story.
Read the excerpt and explain how the setting influences the plot.

> The cave was dark, so dark that Ernesto could not see a thing. He could not see his hand in front of him. He was lost, and he knew that time was running out. He could hear the trickle of water somewhere in the distance. He knew he had to follow the sound. It was his only hope of escaping.

The setting of the cave creates a conflict since Ernesto cannot see a thing and is lost. The excerpt also says that Ernesto's time is running out. While the reader does not know why this is the case, this increases the tension in the story. The fact that Ernesto can hear the dripping of the water is also important to the plot, since it influences the events of the story. Ernesto decides he should go towards the sound of the water. Setting influences the plot here because it creates a struggle for the main character. It also influences the character since Ernesto makes choices about what he should do based on the setting.

Impact of the order of a story or introduction of characters has on a story

The way in which an author chooses to order the events of or introduce characters in a story has a strong effect on it. Most stories are told in chronological order; one event occurs after another. But, an author can influence the development of a story by placing one event out of order to emphasize its importance. Another technique used by some authors is a flashback, in which time changes from the present to the past. When it comes to introducing characters, authors have a great deal of latitude.

- 4 -

Authors often introduce the most important characters first so that the reader will have time to get acquainted with the characters' past and present situations. Readers are often influenced by the author's feelings toward a particular character, which often have an effect on how a character is introduced.

Determining the meaning of words or phrases as they are used in a text

When the reader does not understand a word or a phrase that is used in a passage or a story, it is important to examine the context clues around the word or phrase that provide hints about its meaning. Many words have more than one meaning, and it is only through an examination of the context that the reader can figure out the correct meaning. The word "crown" is a good example. This word has several meanings, including a coronet, the top of a head, the act of awarding something to someone, or even the act of hitting someone. Therefore, it is important to understand the context. In the sentence, "He sought to be crowned the winner of the competition," it is clear that the meaning is "to be awarded." Context must also be used to determine the meaning of phrases. In the sentence, "He wasn't going to stand for that anymore, so he told his boss off," the reader can use context to get a sense of the meaning of "going to stand for." In this case, the phrase means "not put up with."

Figurative use of a word

Authors use literary devices like figurative language to expand reality in a vivid way. An author can utilize figurative language to connect things in an exaggerated way, which results in a stronger, more vivid image. Examples of figurative language include simile, metaphor, personification, and hyperbole. Similes compare things using the comparing words *like* or *as*. "She is as brave as a lion" is an example of a simile. Metaphors compare things without using comparing words. An example of a metaphor is "She is a lion in the wild." Personification attributes human traits to an animal or non-living thing. "Time flew by" is an example of personification. Hyperbole is an exaggeration that is not believable. "He waited in line for years" is an example of this literary device.

Read the excerpt; identify the form of figurative language represented by the phrase "like a fresh April shower," and explain your answer.

> We had been sequestered inside the barn all afternoon. It was hot, really hot. When the sun finally set and I opened the door, the evening air swept over us like a fresh April shower, leaving us ready to enjoy the evening.

The phrase "like a fresh April shower" is an example of a simile. The phrase compares the air with a fresh April shower and uses the word "like," so it qualifies as a simile. Similes compare two things using the word "like" or "as." This phrase is not a metaphor. Although it compares two things, it uses the word "like"; metaphors do not use either "like" or "as" to compare two things. It is not an example of personification, because nothing is being given human traits. There is no sign of hyperbole here either; there is no sense of an exaggeration.

Relationship between the denotative and connotative meaning of words

The denotative meaning of a word and the connotative meaning are only alike in that, according to the dictionary, they mean the same thing. However, that is where the similarities end. The connotative meaning of a word is what is suggested above and beyond the literal meaning. For instance, the word "untidy" might mean "messy" or "unclean," whereas the word "slovenly" suggests something closer to "filthy." When writers create stories, they frequently use words that have strong connotations to describe and develop the characters and the setting. It is important for the reader to analyze these word choices to gain a better understanding of the author's purpose.

Read the following sentence.

> I expected my gear to be inspected, but I never thought it would be scrutinized to this degree.

Explain the connotative meanings of the word "scrutinized" and how they relate to the word "inspected."

Both "scrutinized" and "inspected" have the dictionary meaning of being "closely looked at" or "studied." But, the word "scrutinized" means that something is being dissected and analyzed, not just inspected or checked out. The word "scrutinized" is a much stronger term than the word "inspected." Many things are inspected, but not everything is scrutinized. It is important to choose words that fit the situation, something that is done in this sentence. The connotations that a word brings to a sentence will impact the way a reader comprehends what is being written about. Words with strong connotations help a reader get a feel for what is being written about.

Impact of words on tone

Words can have a large impact on the tone of a passage. Tone is a result of the choice of language. For instance, when talking about or suggesting the mood of a person or a setting, it is vital to choose the right language to describe it. Is a person ecstatic, or is the person simply content? Is a room barren, or is it just empty? Similarly, using strong action verbs can create a tone that is forceful and remembered easily. The verb *buttress*, for instance, has a much stronger impact than the verb *strengthen*. Even though both words have basically the same meaning, the first one creates a more vivid image in the mind of the reader. It is important to use words that will be understood by the audience and will have the desired effect.

Fresh and engaging language

One way to get a reader's attention and hold it is to use language that is fresh and engaging. Using a personal point of view is a good way to accomplish this. You should try to generate excitement by using a different perspective. Always avoid clichés—they will come across as stale and worn out. Learning editing skills is useful; it will help you eliminate unnecessary portions of a text. Use a dictionary and a thesaurus to locate the words you are looking for, and analyze the words to determine how a reader might perceive them. Finally, read your passage aloud to see how it sounds.

Read the excerpt. Describe why the language is fresh and engaging.

> "Full many a glorious morning have I seen
> Flatter the mountain tops with sovereign eye,
> Kissing with golden face the meadows green,
> Gilding pale streams with heavenly alchemy;"
> (Shakespeare, Sonnet XXXIII)

In these few lines, Shakespeare provides the reader with a fresh, new image of nature. Morning is personified as a romantic king in love with the meadows and streams. It is not just any morning, but *a glorious morning*, and it makes the mountain tops look even better than usual. Alchemy was a combination of magic and science thought to enable the creation of precious gold from ordinary metals, and the excerpt describes the streams as gilded, or covered with gold. The king himself is *kissing with golden face*. The lines are simple, and at the same time, sweet and poetic. The sun is the ruler of all. The writing is fresh and engaging.

Comedic or tragic resolution

When an author decides to include a comedic or tragic resolution in a story, the author is using a time-tested literary form that has existed for hundreds, even thousands, of years. The tragedy has a strict format. There is a tragic hero or protagonist who has a fatal flaw and becomes victim to it in the end. The play or story always ends sadly, with the hero in most cases dying or coming to some terrible end. A comedic resolution, on the other hand, always includes a happy ending. There are playful aspects to the plot and the ways in which the characters interact. These literary forms tell the reader what to expect in the story and how to assess the plot. They act as signposts as a reader proceeds through a text.

Understatement or a sense of irony

Many authors enjoy using a sense of irony or understatement as they write a story. Both techniques distance the writer from the characters and the events of a story. In either case, the reader must read between the lines to figure out what the author is actually getting at and what his or her point of view actually is. Understatement can be used as a humorous vehicle, allowing the author to comment on what is happening without being deeply emotionally invested in it. Irony allows the author to make a statement about what is really occurring without openly stating it. When reading a text, be sure to look for any underlying meaning that an author might be trying to convey. An initial reading of a text may not be enough to discern its true intended meaning. The way an author talks about what is happening often conveys that author's viewpoint of the events.

Satire vs. sarcasm

Satire exposes the follies, foibles, and traditions of society, and is often humorous. A satire critiques the pretensions of powerful people in society. While criticism is intended, it is not overt, but rather implied. Mark Twain often employed satire to make a comment about the society in which his characters lived. Sarcasm is a type of humor that is meant to be insulting. Satire may employ the literary technique of irony, which is the tension between what is expected and what actually happens. Sarcasm is a sharp, bitter comment or remark that may or may not utilize understatement. It is an obvious criticism, and does not have the sophistication or creativity of satire, which is usually associated with an entire work. Sarcasm is usually limited to a comment.

Distinguishing between an author's point of view and what they may say literarily about a character or a situation

An author may use a wide array of literary techniques to discuss a topic, a character, or a situation, which could disguise the author's real feelings regarding what he or she is writing about. For instance, a writer might say that an area received a "little rain," when in fact the land might be flooded with water. Or, an author could describe a dent as "a little scratch" when there is actually an enormous dent. A reader must be able to put a writer's words into perspective to determine what has actually occurred.

The same is true when a writer uses irony to make a comment. Consider the following sentence: "I have little doubt that you will receive the praise that you deserve for your hard work." Taken at face value, this would be a compliment. However, if the situation is such that the recipient of the comment has made a complete fool of himself, the comment becomes irony, because the opposite of what is being said is true. Here again, the reader has to be careful to examine a situation described by a writer before jumping to conclusions about the author's viewpoint.

Ways in which Shakespeare's *Romeo and Juliet* is a timeless story

The story of a young man and woman falling in love and coming to a tragic end has been told over and over, and it represents a universal theme in literature. It was originally told by the Roman writer Ovid in his play *Pyramus and Thisbe*, which is a story of forbidden love. In modern times, a musical with a plot similar to *Romeo and*

Juliet is *West Side Story*, which was in fact based on Shakespeare's play. It's important to note, however, that the theme was explored even before Shakespeare wrote his tragedy. Universal themes are found throughout literature. Even the Disney movie *Lady and the Tramp* has elements of the story of ill-fated love that is recounted in *Romeo and Juliet*.

In what way is *Antigone* by the Greek writer Sophocles related to Henry David Thoreau's essay "Civil Disobedience"? In *Antigone*, the title character defies Creon, the ruler of Thebes, by invoking divine justice and breaking Creon's law to bury her brother. In his essay, Thoreau argues that people have a right and responsibility to rebel against laws that are immoral.

They are related because they share a universal theme of rebelliousness against laws that are unjust. Much of literature contains universal themes that repeat situations and ideals that humans live by. The fact that Antigone went against Creon shows that she had moral courage; the same is true of Thoreau, who argued against laws that were unjust. Even though *Antigone* is a play and was written long ago, it still relates to Thoreau's essay, which was written in the 19th century. Universal themes are timeless and are often repeated, but the context in which they are presented is affected by the times in which they are written.

Both Henry David Thoreau and Nathaniel Hawthorne were American writers of the 19th century. Thoreau's essays focused on the quiet desperation of man. Hawthorne's novels focused on characters who were struggling with the Puritanical background of America. Discuss the ways in which their viewpoints were different.

Thoreau was part of the Transcendental Movement that was awakening during the 19th century. It held that nature was a vital part of the human experience. Unlike the Puritanical viewpoint that people had little control over their destiny, the Transcendentalists believed that humans could choose their destiny. Thoreau was writing from this viewpoint, while Hawthorne was more concerned with the Puritanical legacy, which allowed little room for change or imagination. His books were a comment on this strict background, while Thoreau's essays were an exploration of a new world. Even though they wrote during the same century, their works represented different understandings of man's position in the universe.

Upton Sinclair's novel The Jungle is about an immigrant family's experiences working in a factory; John Steinbeck's novel The Grapes of Wrath is about a family of migrant workers suffering in the Dust Bowl of Middle America. They were both written in the early 20th century. Discuss why these authors most likely decided to write about these subjects.

These authors wrote about poor people in difficult situations; they were both concerned about social problems. This is a common theme of early 20th century literature, when the concept of helping the poor worker was just being introduced. One writer spoke of an immigrant family. The other based his novel on a migrant family. They would have had a lot in common, since both families were without roots. This theme is typical of the literature of the early 20th century, when so many immigrants were pouring into the United States. It was also timely because there were few laws restricting the kind of work that migrants could do

Importance of being able to read and comprehend a wide variety of texts by the end of grade 11 and grade 12

It is important for an 11th grader to be able to read and comprehend literature—including stories, dramas, and poetry—in order to be well-versed in literature and how it reflects the various periods in which it was written. The student will develop a good background in the cultural aspects of writing, and will know how to respond to cultural references found in texts. The ability to read and comprehend literature will also help the student prepare for his or her future academic and career path.

The reasons why it is important for a student to be able to comprehend a wide variety of texts by the end of the 12th grade are manifold. This background will give the student a great advantage in terms of achieving success in school and the business world. Being widely read ensures greater knowledge of the world, helps a student become well-versed in cultural differences, and also gives the student a chance to develop his or her vocabulary and ability to express her or himself. Ultimately, having read a large number of different literary books will educate the student in many fields, and will help her or him become confident in our ever-complicated world, where communication is vital.

Informational Texts

Inference

An inference is a conclusion you can make based on the evidence in a passage. For instance, if a passage says that there are many people who ride bicycles to work, and that many people prefer riding a bike to driving a car, you might make the conclusion that riding a bike is fun. This is based on the information that you have on hand; it could be wrong, but it is the best guess you can make. Inferences need to have evidence that they are the most likely outcome. In this case, the fact that many people prefer riding a bike to work over driving a car leads the reader to conclude that riding a bike is fun.

Identify the information in the following excerpt that supports the inference that aluminum is a good material for a boat.
> Cement is heavy, and it can support weight. But, it sinks in water. Aluminum is light, and it does not rust easily. It floats easily. Bricks are made up of clay that is fired. They are fire resistant, and they last a long time. But, bricks are heavy.

The information that supports the inference that aluminum is a good material for a boat is that it is light and does not rust easily. Another supporting detail is that it floats easily. This is what the excerpt says. And this is the kind of evidence that is needed to support the inference identified in the question. The other details describe other materials, but they do not give information that suggests these materials would be good for a boat. Inferences are the best conclusions that can be made based on the information at hand.

Determining the central ideas of a passage

Central ideas are what a passage is mainly about. They are why the passage is written. The main idea is often found in a topic sentence or even a concluding sentence, and there are supporting details found in the passage that expand upon the main idea. There can, however, be more than one central idea, and these main ideas can be related and intertwined. For instance, the main or central idea of a passage may be that rainforests are drying out. A related main idea might be that the result of rainforest destruction is a loss of wildlife. These two central ideas are obviously related, and the passage may present both of them by focusing on one in one part of the passage and the other in another part of the passage. Another way they could be related is in a cause and effect relationship, with the loss of rainforests being the reason for losses of wildlife. It is important to always check to see if there is more than one central idea in a passage.

Read the excerpt below. Identify and discuss the main idea.

> Students who have jobs while attending high school tend not to have as much time to complete their homework as other students. They also do not have time for other activities. We should try to persuade our young people to concentrate on doing well in school, not to concentrate on making money. Having a job while you are a student is harmful.

The main idea of the excerpt is actually the last sentence: "Having a job while you are a student is harmful." This is what the excerpt is mostly about. The other sentences contain supporting information: students who have jobs don't have as much time for homework; students with jobs don't have time for as many activities. These are both supporting details that tell more about the main idea. The third sentence deals with a persuasive argument; it is another kind of detail. Only the last sentence tells what the excerpt is mostly about. Main ideas are sometimes found in a topic sentence at the start of a text or in the concluding sentence, which is the case in this excerpt.

Summary of an informational text

A summary of an informational text should include the main idea or ideas of the passage and also the pertinent supporting details. A summary should not be a vague statement about what a passage is about, but should include important facts, events, or evidence that make the text a complete work. In order to write an objective summary, you need to think about what the text is saying, and then create a precise outline of the main idea and the important supporting information. Summarizing is not the same as paraphrasing. Paraphrasing involves rewording the main idea and supporting ideas in a fairly detailed way; summarizing does not. Summaries afford the reader the opportunity to quickly review the main points of a passage and the important details.

Analyzing a text

When you read a text, you need to pay attention. You need to watch for the introduction of ideas. You need to figure out how the ideas that are introduced are developed. When you read a complex text, it may be difficult to follow. Sometimes, it is hard to understand how one idea is linked to another idea. Sometimes, it helps to make an outline of a text. This will help you identify the main ideas. Then, you can figure out which ideas are supporting details. A complex text may also have vocabulary that you cannot understand. If you cannot figure out the meaning of certain words from the context, you can make a list of these words. Then, look them up in a dictionary. This will help you understand the meaning of the text.

Even an informational text tells a story. It introduces information, ideas, individuals, or events, and then provides details about them. A careful reader must learn to figure out the relationships between the details that an author includes and the ideas that the author introduced earlier in the text. Some of the information that is added may be used to supplement the description of an individual, an event, or an idea. Other information may be used to criticize an event, an idea, or an individual. It is up to the reader to have a discerning eye and decide what direction an author is taking by analyzing the author's language and viewpoint, as well as other information.

Meaning of words and phrases

The meaning of words and phrases can typically be determined from the context of the sentence in which they appear, as well as the surrounding sentences. It may be necessary to read an entire text to figure out the meaning of a term, particularly a technical or legal term. While words may be used in a literal manner, phrases can be more difficult to figure out since their meaning is often not tied to the exact meaning of the words that comprise them. Phrases are often expressions that need to be interpreted. Expressions are idioms that are usually part of the vernacular of a language. They may require more effort to understand, although the meaning can often still be gleaned from the context.

Discuss the meaning of the phrase "jump ship" in the following sentence.

> The start-up company wasn't working out the way that Hal and his partner hoped, and they thought it was time to jump ship and get into another business.

To figure out the meaning of the phrase "jump ship," the reader needs to look for context clues in the same way he or she would to figure out the meaning of a single word. The sentence says that the start-up company wasn't working out. It says that Hal and his partner thought it was time to get into another business. You can tell from the context of the sentence that the expression "jump ship" means to get out of something or to quit something. It has nautical overtones, and it comes from a nautical saying, but the context of the sentence makes it clear what the expression, or idiom, means. Although it might seem to have negative connotations, it does not necessarily have to be negative. It is a kind of final act, which could be construed as negative. However, the context of the sentence suggests that "jumping ship" in this instance might result in something positive occurring.

Read the excerpt below. Use the context clues to decide what the word "Waterloo" means in this instance.

> Connie was worried that the competition was her Waterloo. She realized she wasn't Napoleon and she wasn't losing her entire kingdom because she lost a battle, but that's how it felt to her.

Using context clues is a good way to figure out the meanings of words and expressions without having to look them up in a dictionary. The way to discover context clues is to study the text. The excerpt says that Connie was worried that the competition was her Waterloo. This is obviously a reference to something, but it takes further analysis to figure out what it means. The next sentence talks about Napoleon and how he lost a kingdom because of a battle. One can draw the conclusion that "Waterloo" was probably the battle, and that someone's Waterloo is something that a person loses or does badly in. This helps the reader figure out the meaning of the word.

Figurative language

Figurative language is language that is used in a non-literal way. It allows the writer to expand the ways in which he or she uses language, making it more colorful and fresh. Figurative language takes a word or an expression that has a literal meaning and gives it a new one. For instance, an author might say that Lilli is like a graceful swan. While everyone knows that Lilli is a person, the image of Lilli as a graceful swan casts a new descriptive meaning. Figurative language takes many forms; it can be in the form of a simile, a metaphor, personification, or hyperbole. Similes compare things using the comparing words "*like*" or "*as.*" An example is, "Lilli is like a graceful swan." Metaphors compare things without using comparing words. An example is, "Lilli is a swan when she moves." Personification attributes human traits to an animal or an inanimate object. An example is, "The swan spoke to Lilli."

Read the excerpt from former President George W. Bush's Second Inaugural Address.

"...By our efforts, we have lit a fire as well - a fire in the minds of men. It warms those who feel its power, it burns those who fight its progress, and one day this untamed fire of freedom will reach the darkest corners of our world."

Discuss the metaphor that former President Bush uses in this excerpt.

The metaphor that President Bush uses is that of a fire of freedom that will grow in the minds of men and will warm those who feel its power. This fire is powerful, according to the metaphor, since it would burn those who fight against freedom. It is also powerful because it will reach all over the world. Bush uses the metaphor of a fire since it suggests light, and democracy is a kind of light that allows people to see the truth. That is why the metaphor is a powerful one. This is an example of how strong a metaphor can be in terms of getting a person's viewpoint and thoughts across to the public.

Aggressive vs. assertive connotations

The words "aggressive" and "assertive" both describe someone with a strong nature. However, the word "aggressive" suggests someone who may be hostile or belligerent, while the term "assertive" could be interpreted to mean self-confident or self-assured. "Aggressive" has negative connotations when used to describe someone's nature, while the word "assertive" has more positive connotations. These words are examples of differences in connotations, since they both have meanings that go beyond what appears in the dictionary. Words like these should be chosen carefully, since they can convey a message about someone that may or may not be intended. When choosing words, a writer needs to look for the most accurate word to describe a person or a thing.

Author's point of view

When an author writes a text, he or she must choose the structure that will work best for the text. For informational passages, there are several different structures an author can use. These include question and answer order, chronological or sequential order, problem and solution order, cause and effect order, and spatial order. Some texts use a combination of two or more of these structures depending on the breakdown of the topic. For persuasive documents, a question and answer order is often a good choice because it allows for a dramatic presentation of materials. This structure allows the author to highlight arguments for or against a position. A cause and effect order structure might also be a good choice for a persuasive text, and would also allow for the highlighting of arguments, as would a problem and solution order. Compare and contrast and order of importance are reasonable choices for informational pieces, and possibly for persuasive texts as well. Chronological ordering would be more suitable for an informational piece on a person or an event, where the points that are being made are not meant to convince the reader of something. The author should choose the structure that will best meet his or her writing goals.

Veronica is doing a report on why people should stop the killing of whales. She is trying to figure out which text structure would best help her meet her goal to outline the reasons why this harvesting will result in the loss of species that are important to the environment. Describe which type of order would probably work best for this report, and explain why.

The best possible choices for the report would probably be either a problem and solution or a cause and effect organization, since they would allow the author to lay out the problem and the consequences of the killing of whales. A cause and effect order would show the immediate relationship between the killing of whales and its consequence; a problem and solution order would probably be best if the author wants to concentrate on the ways in which this practice is causing society problems and how the practice could be resolved. A compare and contrast structure would probably not work in this type of report. Finally, a chronological structure, which might be useful in part of the report to outline the past history of the practice, would probably not be a suitable structure for the entire report.

An author's point of view may be clear, or it may be hidden. It is important to read a text closely to find out exactly what the author thinks about the event, person, topic, or issue he or she is writing about. When reading, look for clues to the author's viewpoint in the form of emotional statements or critiques of others discussing the topic. Some authors make their viewpoints known only through rhetorical statements. These need to be analyzed closely to see if they should be taken at face value or if the author is somehow using rhetoric to exaggerate a point or to try to persuade the reader of something. Rhetoric can be a very effective vehicle that can draw a reader in through the use of elegant language. This is precisely why it is important to analyze an author's rhetoric to determine why he or she is employing it and what his or her goal might be. It is also vital to read the entire text before making any assumptions about an author's viewpoint.

The purpose of the rhetoric in the following excerpt from a speech by former President George W. Bush.

> "Our opportunities are too great, our lives too short, to waste this moment. So tonight we vow to our nation. We will seize this moment of American promise. We will use these good times for great goals."

The President's purpose is clear; he wants to set an important goal for the public. In doing so, he is attempting to paint a picture of the importance of what he is saying. Phrases such as "Our opportunities are too great," "We will seize the moment," and "good times for great goals" set the stage for putting forth the President's agenda, which he hopes to present in the best possible light. Words have the capacity to transfix listeners with their elegance, a fact clearly illustrated by this excerpt. That is why speeches are so important to the political arena, and it is why excellent speech writers are extremely important to political candidates.

Using information technology skills wisely

Good information technology skills are necessary in order to sift through the enormous amount of information available on just about any topic. Before beginning any research, ask yourself how much information you think you are going to need; think about your target audience and their needs. Utilize search engines to make the task go faster. When evaluating multiple sources of information, do not rely solely on how recent they are. Consider the validity of sources as well. Do not rely on just one source. Using digital media is important because it allows you to broaden your scope beyond just words to include graphics and charts. Take the time to understand what online sources of information are available, which ones are most appropriate, and how they support one another.

Using the reasoning that the Founding Fathers believed that African Americans could not be viewed as citizens as defined in the U.S. Constitution, and therefore had no rights before the Court, Chief Justice Taney's majority opinion ignited a firestorm of controversy in the already heated debate between pro- and anti-slavery advocates in the United States during the mid-19th century. Many opponents decried the chief justice's ruling as one that was motivated by politics. One result was that the U.S. Congress could no longer regulate slavery anywhere. The Dred Scott Decision is viewed as one of a series of events that eventually pushed the country into the Civil War.

Analyze the following excerpt from Lincoln's Second Inaugural Address in 1865.

> "It may seem strange that any men should dare to ask a just God's assistance in wringing their bread from the sweat of other men's faces, but let us judge not, that we be not judged. The prayers of both could not be answered. That of neither has been answered fully…"

In this excerpt and in the address, Lincoln is talking about slavery. Like the majority of people of his time, Lincoln learned to read by studying the Bible. He makes frequent references to the Bible, and he often uses the rhetoric of the Bible to drive his point home. This is common in 19th century literary documents. When he says, "Wringing their bread from the sweat of other men's faces," he is paraphrasing from the Book of Genesis, which refers to physical work. Here, the word *bread* is used to refer to the wealth of the slave owners. Lincoln finds it strange that these slave owners should pray to the same God as those who do not own slaves for assistance in making money. He encourages his audience not to be hypocritical when he says, "let us judge not." This is a reference to the Book of Matthew of the Bible.

Importance of being a proficient reader of literary nonfiction texts by grade 11 and grade 12

It is extremely important for a student to be proficient in reading literary nonfiction texts by the end of grade 11. These types of texts will play a key role in the student's future life (and success). In other words, the ability to comprehend language and vocabulary will help the student attain the academic level he or she hopes to or the type of employment desired. In all walks of life, people need to be able to read and comprehend a variety of materials. This is why the ability to understand literary nonfiction texts is a valuable tool. It is especially important for those who hope to do well on college entrance examinations as well as other kinds of job examinations.

It is of the utmost importance for a 12th-grade student to be able to read literary nonfiction proficiently. Not only is it important for future academic endeavors (e.g., college and graduate school), but it is also vital to future career success. Whether it is reading a newspaper, an employee manual, or a science text, it is crucial that a person be comfortable when reading and be able to comprehend the material without extreme effort. Without this ability, a person will face limitations in his or her academia and business life. Communication is extremely important in today's workplace, and the foundation of this skill is being able to comprehend reading materials.

Universal themes found in literature are affected by the time in which the literature was written

While universal themes are the same in terms of their meaning and what they depict or teach, the ways in which they are presented are affected by the time in which a literary piece was written. The characters and situations that are portrayed will mirror the environment in which the writer lived. Ancient literature depicts a time when myth was very much alive, and when the concept of personal freedom was still evolving and not taken for granted.

Evaluate the purpose of the following excerpt from George Washington's Farewell Address, which was given on September 19, 1796.

> "The unity of government which constitutes you one people is also now dear to you. It is justly so, for it is a main pillar in the edifice of your real independence, the support of your tranquility at home, your peace abroad; of your safety; of your prosperity; of that very liberty which you so highly prize..."

This address given by the first president of the U.S. when he announced that he did not want to run for re-election went over the groundwork that had established the new country. The passage stresses *the unity of government which constitutes you one people.* Washington truly believed that the U.S. would be able to survive any attack, from without as well as from within, if it stayed with this principle. There is a hint that Washington foresaw the difficulties of holding together *the main pillar* (the different states) that were to come. His farewell address would go on to influence politicians and leaders for many years to come.

Writing

Clear and coherent writing

Clear and coherent writing requires good initial planning. You need to determine what you are going to say, who you are saying it to, and how you want to say it, as well as the kind of tone you want to project. In the process of writing, organize your arguments and use a logical order to develop them. Use paragraph breaks to help organize your thoughts. Your sentences should be precise and to the point. Make sure your punctuation is correct. Your ideas should be supported by evidence, and opposing ideas should be mentioned as well. When you get to your conclusion, avoid being repetitious; concentrate on summarizing. Proofread what you have written to check for any errors; reading the text aloud is often helpful.

Importance of planning, revising, editing, and reviewing a text

Draw up a brief plan before you start to write so that you know what points you are going to cover. Once you have finished the writing, it is a good idea to set it aside for a time. That way, when you look at it again to see if revisions are needed, you will be approaching it with a fresh mind. During the process of editing, make sure you check for any grammatical, spelling, punctuation, or usage errors. Are your supporting details clear and presented in a logical order? Will your audience respond to your text? During your review process, you may feel that some sections need to be rewritten. Think about whatever criticism your peers or adults may have had about previous work as you review your writing.

Read the following passage, explain why it needs to be revised, and discuss how best to revise it.

> Raising a puppy is more difficult. We all know how cute they are. Like kittens, they need a lot of care. So, don't be shocked that I tell you kittens are more cute.

The writer of these sentences has not made it clear what he or she is really trying to say. There is no organization, and there are grammatical and usage errors. A good revision would look like this:

> We all know how cute puppies and kittens are. They both require a lot of care, but I think puppies are more difficult to raise than kittens. I also think that kittens are cuter than puppies.

Here the thoughts are put down in a logical order. The writer makes a statement of fact (*puppies and kittens are cute*), and one of opinion (*I think...*), so it is clear what her preferences are. The passage now makes sense, and the writing is free from errors.

Conducting a research project

When conducting a short or a sustained research project to answer a question or solve a problem, it is a good idea to draw up a plan first. Then, make a list of keywords related to the question or problem. You can utilize these words either in a search engine or an online or print encyclopedia. Back issues of magazines, journals, and newspapers can also be used as source material. If you are synthesizing multiple sources, combine the similarities or the differences you have come up with. It is important that none of the information you gather be dated or untimely. All sources have to be cited following Modern Language Association (MLA) guidelines. Questions raised by your research should be explicit.

Using the internet

Online sources that allow writers to get works published at little to no cost either as an e-book or a printed book are now widely available. There are editing as well as marketing services offered on many Internet sites. Writing tools offer help with everything from style to grammar. Sites for research are reliable, and offer accurate and objective information. Make sure you cite Internet sources using an accepted format such as that from the MLA (Modern Language Association). There are free online tools that can be accessed to allow people to work together on projects no matter how far apart they are geographically. Chat rooms and topic websites allow for an unprecedented exchange of information. Shared writing projects let you get adult input or brainstorm with your peers.

Gathering relevant information from multiple print and digital sources

Before compiling information from multiple print and digital sources, you must first decide how much information you need based on the scope of the project, and you must determine how knowledgeable your audience is. Make an outline of the similarities as well as the differences you encounter in various sources. Journals, text books, magazines, newspapers, and even texts written by other students: the number of sources you can uncover is limited only by your imagination. Strike a balance between being too detailed and bogged down, and too general and oversimplified. Whatever the source, verify how timely, accurate, and credible it is. You can avoid plagiarism, or using another person's words without acknowledgement, by following MLA (Modern Language Association) guidelines when you cite their works.

F. Scott Fitzgerald's novel The Great Gatsby takes place on Long Island (near New York City) in the 1920s, during an era known as the Jazz Age. Discuss what the author's subject reveals about American society at that time.

Fitzgerald was writing about a time when there was a period of great wealth in the country, as well as great excess and abandon, after the end of World War I. He portrays society's fascination with the ideals of wealth and happiness, the so-called "American Dream." The two main characters, Nick and Gatsby, both of whom served their country during the war, are cynical and disillusioned. Gatsby throws lavish parties at his estate every weekend with liquor (outlawed by the Eighteenth Amendment) flowing freely. Fitzgerald captures the mood with striking clarity, portraying the moral emptiness of the time and the growing distrust of the wealthy as the decade careened towards its close with the Great Depression of 1929.

Evaluate the purpose of the following excerpt from Franklin D. Roosevelt's speech of July 2, 1932.

> "I pledge you, I pledge myself, to a new deal for the American people. Let us all here assembled constitute ourselves prophets of a new order of competence and of courage. This is more than a political campaign; it is a call to arms…"

In this speech given by Franklin D. Roosevelt when he accepted the Democratic nomination for President, he proposed launching a new effort to turn back the tide of Depression that had gripped the country for several years. In using the phrase "a call to arms," he addressed the audience in a manner similar to how a commander would address his soldiers. His purpose was to contrast himself and the Democratic Party with the Republican view of government, which favored big businesses and a continuation of the policies of Herbert Hoover. He subsequently went on to win in a landslide victory in November, and his policies, of course, went on to be labeled by history as The New Deal.

Make writing a habit

In today's information driven society, writing is a skill that is of utmost importance in adult life. Writing, whether it is a short paragraph or two or an extended thesis, should come easily and smoothly (and should even be second nature) for those who wish to be successful. As such, writing should become a habit. An adult who follows the old adage "the more you write, the better you write" is sure to achieve recognition in any field of endeavor. It is important to study the writing process—the conscious effort of note taking, writing drafts, editing, and revising—so that you will grasp the concept of fine tuning your writing to different audiences, and will feel equally at ease writing a short note or a thoroughly researched treatise.

Persuasive text

Introducing an argument in a persuasive passage
The best way to introduce an argument in a persuasive passage and to structure it is to begin by organizing your thoughts and researching the evidence carefully. You should write everything down in outline format to start. Make sure you put the

claim at the beginning of the passage. Then, list the reasons and the evidence that you have to support the claim. It is important that you provide enough evidence. Reasons and evidence should follow each other in a logical order. Write the passage so that you hold the reader's attention; use a strong tone and choose words carefully for maximum effect. If you can get the reader to understand your claim, he or she will be more likely to agree with your argument. Restate your claim in the concluding paragraph to maximize the impact on the reader.

Making a claim
When making a claim, it is important to first think about the arguments that support that claim. While researching, try to anticipate what readers might say; this will help you thoroughly develop your claim. It is not enough to research a claim on the Internet, because many sources are dubious at best. Look for sites that are objective. Find authorities that you can quote, and use statistics. Present counterclaims using ample evidence. Mention both the strengths and weaknesses without any prejudice. Divide each counterclaim into a separate paragraph with supporting evidence. Make sure to present everything in a logical manner so that the information will be easily understood by the reader. Most importantly, one needs to separate opinions from facts.

Creating cohesion
The best way to create cohesion between claims and evidence is to organize your ideas, and then write sentences explaining your reasons and evidence that logically follow your main ideas. Careful research will result in your argument being cohesive and easy to understand. Your claim and evidence must be clearly related to each other. Sometimes, it is useful to include metaphors, similes, or analogies to make your point clearer. Words and phrases that will indicate to the reader that the claim and evidence are related include "since," "because," "as a consequence," and "as a result." You can also utilize clauses to demonstrate a relationship between the reason and the effect. This approach is illustrated in the following sentence: "Since the sun now rose earlier in the morning, the birds awakened earlier and began their song." The first clause sets the tone, and it establishes causality between the reason and the effect. After writing, reread your text to verify that the relationships between cause and effect are logical.

Formal style
A formal style is important when you want your writing to be objective and precise. A few requirements must be met to achieve this. It is important not to use fragments; write in complete sentences. Avoid contractions, and do not change tenses between sentences or paragraphs. Do not use the words "I" or "you"; this will add a more serious tone to your writing. Whenever possible, avoid using the passive tense. Using the active voice will make your writing more focused and interesting. Ensure your spelling is correct and that you follow all punctuation rules. Finally, make sure your ideas are presented in a logical order.

Read the following passage and suggest some ways to make it more formal.

When I was a kid growing up, I remember I had a lot of hard times. As a teenager, other kids used to make fun of me and call me names. It was really depressing. I couldn't find anyone to take to the prom. Sometimes, it was hard to keep up with all my homework.

Here is one way to rewrite it:

Becoming a teenager can be a stressful time. Adolescence involves both physical and emotional changes. Peer pressure and pressure at school cause many teenagers to have anxiety disorders; some even suffer from mild to severe depression. Boys and girls both worry about their physical appearance and about being popular.

The account is presented in the third person to make the passage more authoritative and formal. Complex sentences are utilized to keep the writing varied and interesting. Personal emotions are expressed in a more objective manner. A higher level of vocabulary results in a more precise, informed, and impressive finished text.

Concluding statement

A concluding statement is an important part of a persuasive passage because it sets the tone for the reader and adds a sense of completion. A concluding sentence should not just repeat what was already said; the concluding statement should tie everything together. The concluding sentence should basically restate the importance of the argument. By doing this in the concluding paragraph, the impact on the reader will be maximized, and you will be more likely to bring the reader over to your side of an argument. The conclusion should logically fit into the flow of your passage. A good concluding statement serves to cement the bonds you have developed with the reader, and provides one more opportunity to get the reader on your side.

What kind of argument would the following concluding sentence be best suited for?

As a result, soccer is the most popular sport in the world.

The sentence makes a good concluding sentence for a passage about the reasons why soccer (called football outside of the U.S.) is the most popular sport in the world. Arguments can include the fact that players do not need any special equipment, while players of a similar sport—American football—need equipment such as helmets and protective padding. Another good angle is the fact that players don't have to be a certain size to play soccer, whereas the sport of American football places a premium on very large players, especially when filling defensive positions. Basketball, another sport that is also popular, requires a wooden court and two metal baskets with nets installed at a certain height. The concluding sentence provided would tie all the elements of the argument together.

Informational or Explanatory Text

Introducing a topic

An informational or explanatory text should have an introduction to the topic that the text will cover. One way you can accomplish this is by using a topic sentence, with details that support your thesis included afterwards. Another tactic is to use a reference to something going on in the modern world, even if your topic relates to something in the past. This makes your topic immediately more relevant. Some writers like to preview the ideas and concepts they are going to discuss by showing their relevance to a main topic. You could also preview concepts by demonstrating how they relate to everyday life.

Developing a topic

It is important to develop the topic of an informational or explanatory text by utilizing relevant facts that clearly support the main topic. Include a topic sentence followed by any supporting details. These details should preferably be concrete facts that you have carefully researched, and which you are certain are accurate. You can also provide quotes taken from known experts in a field that is relevant to your topic. Quotes not only lend credibility to your thesis, but can also make your writing more varied and interesting. Diverse multimedia techniques, charts, and examples will also enhance your presentation. However, you should make sure these techniques play a supportive role, and are not presented solely to make your text look flashy.

Creating cohesion

Experienced writers know how to use appropriate transitions to create cohesion in a text. They serve to clarify the relationships between ideas and concepts. Transition words or phrases such as "consequently," "therefore," and "as a result of" indicate causality between ideas. "However," "on the other hand," "in contrast," "but," and "similarly" indicate a compare and contrast relationship. You can also draw attention to examples by using words and phrases like "namely," "for example," "for instance," and "that is." When you need to show the order of importance of ideas or concepts, use transitions such as "at first," "primarily," "secondly," "former," or "latter."

Using precise language and domain-specific vocabulary

Writers of informational or explanatory texts must use precise language and domain specific vocabulary in order to accurately get their ideas across. General vocabulary words will not bring home the points you are trying to make. Your audience will not follow your thesis closely if the text lacks the details that are supplied by carefully chosen, precise, and domain specific language. Using the word "isobar" in a text about meteorology, for instance, would be more effective than using the word "pressure." During the research stage, make sure you closely study the vocabulary used. Use a dictionary to clarify the meanings of words and terms you do not understand.

Establishing and maintaining a formal style

Experienced writers use a formal style when they are writing explanatory or informational texts to lend greater credence to their material. They do not use an informal or colloquial tone, and they utilize the third person for objectivity. They use complex sentences, which are longer and add a further tone of formality and depth to the subject. By using a formal style, they show that they are serious about their subject. They are striving to make supporting details clear and to the point, but they are also presenting them in as much complexity as the intended audience can absorb. There is no introduction of personal opinion, unless that opinion can be carefully justified.

Importance of a good concluding statement

A good concluding statement should sum up the overall intention of the text, and serves to "wrap up" the passage so that the reader is aware that you arrived at the logical ending of your argument. The conclusion should review the most salient points that you made, the reasoning you employed, and the supporting arguments for your reasoning. It serves to reinforce in the reader's mind that you did not leave anything out. The reader should not feel that there is more pertinent information that may follow. A good conclusion allows the reader to sit back and weigh the overall impact of your thesis, and it greatly increases the effectiveness of a text.

Narratives

Setting the stage

To set the stage for a narrative, you need to introduce the reader to the setting and the characters. Next, you should introduce a plot line. This should consist of various events that lead to a problem, a climax, and a resolution. This gives a narrative structure. The way in which the author introduces these elements has an influence on the overall effectiveness of the narrative. Make sure to use language to describe the setting and the characters that will grab the reader's attention. Make the details specific. The conclusion or resolution will allow you to tie up the details of the story.

Introducing a narrator

The narrator in a story is the person doing the "speaking," or the one who is telling the story. A narrator can speak in the first or third person. The narrator can shift from one person to another during the course of the story. It is even possible for the narrator to be non-human. The introduction of your narrator can be quick, subtle, dramatic, or humorous; it is up to you. Many times, an event or a circumstance opens the story. Make sure any details about time, place, and circumstance are developed logically and naturally, and that the reader will understand who (or what) the narrator is and where the narrator fits into the story.

Using techniques

Writers employ numerous techniques to bring a narrative to life. Dialogue is one tool; it gives the reader a sense of what is happening, and also adds color and nuance to characters or the narrator. What a character says and how he says it portrays how that character feels. Pacing is also used in a narrative. The rhythms of the sentences, whether they are short or long, allow a writer to use time to the best effect, and to add color and depth to the events in the narrative. The plot line or sequence of events in the narrative is the actual structure of the story, and is developed from the opening of the story through one or more actions. These actions eventually lead to a climax, and then a resolution. The use of descriptions lets the reader visualize what is happening.

Interjecting sequence

Sequence should come in an order that can be easily grasped by the reader. It is a function of a natural flow of events, dialogue, and plot. Sequence should enhance what is happening in the story, and it should never seem forced or unnatural. A pattern should emerge, and it must make sense to the reader. Often times, a writer will make use of a flashback, a literary device where the writer goes back in time, and where events do not follow in sequence. When crafted properly, the flashback will make sense in the context of the story. Flashbacks can often add a sense of mystery or suspense to a narrative. Chronological narration, which puts events in the order in which they happened, is another literary device, and is used more frequently than flashbacks.

Using precise language

Precise language is important in a narrative. It helps ensure that the concepts you are trying to communicate are readily understood by the audience. Precise language will be livelier, and will provoke more thought on the part of the reader. It includes the proper use of dialogue and imagery to get the point of the story across as succinctly as possible, so that there is nothing vague in the narrative. Your use of language should show an articulate grasp and control of the plot, and the whole text should be cohesive. Sensory language (which brings up images of the senses) can add extra detail and feeling, and can be very persuasive. Understanding the full range of language will result in a better narrative.

Importance of the conclusion

The conclusion to a narrative is extremely important. An inadequate or poorly thought out conclusion can leave the reader confused and unable to tie everything together, or "wrap things up." There must be some type of resolution to whatever was described in the opening and the events that followed. A conclusion is not repetition; it is resolution. The resolution can be a summary. It could be a quotation. The resolution does not have to be clear cut. In fact, it may leave a lot unanswered. It could end with a rhetorical question or questions. Indeed, unlike traditional writing, conclusions in modern literature often present more questions than answers. In every case, however, the conclusion will leave the reader with no doubt that the narrative is over.

Doreen is writing a short story about training her dog Lola to compete in an agility competition. She has written about all that she has done to train her dog over the past three months. She is preparing to write a conclusion to her story. Describe what Doreen should try to accomplish with her conclusion.

Doreen should write a conclusion to tie everything together. Since she was training her dog Lola to compete, the end of the story should tell whether Lola won the competition. Doreen should describe the day of the competition and the result. This is the most obvious conclusion for her story. Doreen should bring her story to a close with a fitting and appropriate ending so that the reader will know exactly what the outcome was, and will not be left hanging in the end. The opening and all the events that happened lead up to this, and there is a form to her story.

Speaking and Listening

Discussions

Preparing for a discussion on a particular topic

It is exceedingly important to prepare for class discussions. These discussions are important because they help prepare students for future discussions, and also allow them to practice effective techniques and learn communication skills. The exchanging of ideas is a skill that will remain with a student throughout his or her lifetime. When preparing for such a discussion, a student should research the subject at hand using the Internet and other sources. They should make sure they have read all essential applicable information. It is also important to have the resources (quotes, statistics, and audio visual material) you will need during the discussion on hand. A useful technique is to rehearse your role; practice the day before with a family member or a friend. Determine what you are going to focus on. If you are leading the discussion, think ahead about how you are going to guide the discussion to a conclusion, and how much time will be needed.

Rules for collegial discussions

Properly organized collegial discussions can be very productive, and can result in many new and interesting ideas being formulated and brought out in the classroom. It is important that rules be set up to promote civil, democratic discussions. Guidelines for the discussion should be established, which should include how much time each participant will be allowed to talk and then respond. There should be clear roles. Specific goals need to be established, and the progress towards reaching those goals should be tracked, with a deadline for completion kept in mind. Participants should learn how to use questions to add detail and depth to the discussion, and how to build on and further ideas that are put forth by others. It is important to try to understand and communicate with individuals who have a different perspective, especially from a cultural point of view. Everyone should be able to make use of evidence, and should be able to express themselves clearly within the structured framework.

Ways to pose questions that elicit elaboration

Asking questions that will encourage a response from others and propel a conversation entails asking specific, not general, questions, since they force the listener to think. Ideally, questions should be open-ended (i.e. they can't be answered with a simple "yes" or "no"). It is important to be proficient at asking questions, and at learning the art of asking the right question. Being a good listener is key to asking good questions. You should build on the ideas expressed by others in the classroom. One technique is asking a question at the end of what you have to say. You could ask something like, "Does that answer your question?" This helps personalize questions. Another overlooked technique is to take notes. It is also important to prevent people from straying from the subject by taking control of the situation and diplomatically steering the conversation back to the subject at hand.

Ensuring that a full range of positions are equally covered

Guidelines for the discussion should stress allowing each member of the team to express his or her viewpoint without prejudice. Each member should receive the same amount of time to put forth a theory or thesis, or to address a subject through an analytical probe without interruption. On the other hand, every team member should also be granted time to respond to individual presentations. Emotional outbursts do not have a place in this kind of discussion, nor do personal comments that pull away from an objective and intelligent discussion. When there is a divergence of opinion, the greatest of respect should be given to the opposing viewpoints.

Respond to diverse perspectives

Key to responding to diverse perspectives is listening and keeping an open mind. Divergent ideas could be compiled by the entire discussion group in a list. Then, the link between the ideas could be identified, and it might be determined through consensus which opinions require more scrutiny or research. A goal should be set for the investigation or task, and assignments made so that any further research that is needed is done. The conversation can then resume with this new additional information kept in mind. This process is an orderly means of reaching a deeper understanding of a topic that not everyone may agree with or about.

Integrating various sources of information that are presented in diverse formats and media

There are many different sources of information. On the Internet, there are multiple sites (some more reliable than others) where print information as well as charts and other graphic organizers are available to all. In addition, there are hard copy and online journals, textbooks, magazines, and newspapers; researchers are often overwhelmed with information. It is best to choose only the sources that can be verified or are from a credible author or organization. This information must then be analyzed to see how consistent it is and whether valid discrepancies exist, and why. After, it can be used in a presentation or a discussion.

Analyzing a speaker's point of view

The point of view of a speaker needs to be determined to evaluate whether there is a clear delineation between evidence and the speaker's theory. If a speaker's viewpoint is prejudiced or based on emotion, this needs to be identified by evaluating the evidence. It is important to evaluate a speaker's choice of words and tone to determine whether the speech is tinged with feeling or objective. The evidence that a speaker uses to back up claims must also be closely evaluated to determine its source and validity. Many speakers are able to influence an audience through their strength of delivery, but if studied, there may be holes in logic or faults in the evidence that is used to prove a point.

<u>Presenting claims, findings, and supporting evidence</u>
When in a focused discussion, be prepared to present your claims, findings, and supporting evidence in a clear and distinct manner. This means being prepared. When compiling your data, make sure to create an outline that has the main ideas and then the supporting evidence, including graphics that you want to present. Attention to details will result in a successful presentation, one in which the diverse individuals in the group will come away with a feeling of having been part of something meaningful. Facts and examples should be stressed. Repetition creates retention. It is important for the speaker to choose the right words, and to build momentum by gradually building up to the strongest argument(s). Graphics are important, because participants will be more convinced if they can see evidence as well as hear it. By breaking up the flow of the discussion and introducing pauses before and after pertinent arguments, the speaker will make the presentation of facts more interesting.

Presentations

One way to bring a presentation to life is to use digital media, including graphics, audio, visual, and interactive elements. Such tools will not only make a presentation more interesting and memorable, but will also keep those listening from distancing themselves from the presentation. It is easy for audience members to become bored during a presentation if they don't feel included. Digital media can effectively hold their interest. Graphics, diagrams, charts, and maps all serve to reinforce the point you are trying to make. The simpler these forms of media are, the more effective they will be. They serve to help the audience understand your argument; a video or audio can enhance the claims and findings of a presentation. Both visuals and multimedia components should be considered aids; they are not going to do the work for you. It is useful to rehearse the presentation until it flows smoothly.

When giving a speech, you need to make sure you feel confident in front of your audience. Exchange nerves for a funny story to open; have a variety of multimedia graphics that will pull your audience in. Perhaps most important, use the English language correctly when you speak. This is a situation where using correct grammar is essential. Before you speak, write your speech out and make sure that it demonstrates a command of correct conventions. In addition, be sure to speak clearly and slowly, and to enunciate words. Make sure the words that you choose have the correct literal meaning and the intended connotations. Try to avoid hesitations that end with "uh" or "er," which only distract from what you are saying. Look at one person in the audience and talk to her or him. Maintaining a smile will help create an atmosphere of informality. Extra effort needs to be made to avoid being wordy. Redundancy is sure to make audience attention wander.

Eye contact is one of the most important tactics for an effective presentation. When you maintain eye contact with audience members, you can be assured that your listeners will find your presentation believable. They will also be more likely to remember what you said. Reading a speech instead of giving one will have little impact on your audience. Make sure to look people in the eyes and smile. Use a voice that can be easily heard, and enunciate words so people will not be left wondering what was said. Remember to adapt your voice to the task at hand. Are you trying to persuade, look for sympathy, or tell an amazing story? All of these scenarios should yield a different voice and way of presenting the material. Most important of all, relax!

Language

Usage is a matter of convention

Latin is an ancient language. It does not change. But English, like any modern language, may change over time. New words are always being introduced into the English language. Words are adapted from other languages. Examples of adapted words are taco, pizza, and karaoke. Usage, which is a matter of convention, can also change and evolve over time. It is not always clear what the correct form is, since there are sometimes two possibilities. For instance, the use of the subjunctive is much less prevalent today than it was in the past. The answer to the question of whether it is acceptable to begin a question with the word "and" or "but" has also changed. Years ago, this was strictly against usage rules, but it is now common practice in less formal texts.

Use of the serial comma

The rules regarding use of the serial comma differ depending on whether a text is academic or more informal. Traditionally, and in academia, a comma is always used before the "and" in a list of items. This is not the case in more casual texts, such as newspapers, where the convention is not to use a comma before the word "and" in a list of items. This is just one example of how usage conventions are not always rigid, and can change according to the usage of the moment. A general rule of thumb is that a comma should be used in front of the "and" in a list of items if the text is for a school-related or academic use, but should not be used if the text is intended for everyday use.

Marina and Keegan are writing a report together. They are having a disagreement about whether a split infinitive Marina used in one sentence is grammatically correct. Marina thinks the split infinitive is fine in this instance, but Keegan does not agree. How can they come to a resolution about this issue?

There are many grey areas related to English usage, and split infinitives is one of them. The strict notion that they should never be used is less in vogue today than it was a few years ago, and they may now even be found in formal writing. However, if the text that is being prepared is academic, it is probably best to avoid using them. In English, it is always possible to word things differently to avoid awkward usage, and this is also true for split infinitives. Marina and Keegan could consult *Merriam-Webster's Dictionary of English Usage* or *Garner's Modern American Usage* to figure out what they should do. Typically, however, the more academic the paper, the more formal the usage should be.

Rules of hyphenation

Hyphens are used in many instances. They are used to join compound words, whether nouns or verbs. The best way to determine if a word needs a hyphen is to check it in the dictionary. They are used to separate two or more adjectives when they come before a noun. They are used to hyphenate all compound numbers from *twenty-one* through *ninety-nine*. They are used to hyphenate all spelled-out fractions. They are used to hyphenate prefixes when they come before proper nouns. They are used to hyphenate all words beginning with *self* except *selfish* and *selfless*. They are used in some titles, such as vice-president. It is important not to confuse a hyphen with a dash.

Correct the punctuation in the following sentence.

> The forty year old man jumped over the bramble covered fence rail, where he came upon a too good to be true treasure chest filled with gold pieces that were really chocolate candies.

The correct way to write this sentence is: The forty-year-old man jumped over the bramble-covered fence rail, where he came upon a too-good-to-be-true treasure chest filled with gold pieces that were really chocolate candies.

Hyphens are used to join several adjectives modifying a noun when they cannot be joined by the word "and." "Forty," "year," and "old" all modify man and are hyphenated; these modifiers cannot be joined by "and." The same is true of "bramble covered." It would be awkward to say bramble and covered. The two words work together to create a description, so they are hyphenated. The last group of adjectives is "too," "good," and "to be true," which is really an expression that needs to be hyphenated. It is important not to confuse a hyphen with a dash; a dash is used to punctuate clauses, not adjectives. Although not shown here, hyphens are also used to punctuate titles such as "vice-president."

Correct the spelling in the sentence below.

> The visitors will aclimate to the enviromment as soon as they become accustomed to the surroundings of the tropacs.

The words that are misspelled are "aclimate," which should be "acclimate"; "enviromment," which is spelled "environment"; and "tropacs," which is spelled "tropics." It is important to learn to spell words correctly. One way to learn how to spell words is to learn how to sound out words. Break longer words down into syllables, and into affixes and roots. Get the correct spelling from a dictionary, and then practice that spelling. Practice with a few words at a time; use them in sentences. Then move on to new vocabulary words. It is also useful to remember spelling rules, such as "i before e except after c" (receive), "drop the final e" (like, liking), and "double the last consonant" when adding suffixes (stop, stopped).

Syntax

Syntax is the order of the words in a sentence. When writing, it is important to make sure not only that the syntax is correct, but also that it is not repetitive. There is nothing worse than reading a passage that has sentences that are all alike: noun, verb, object. These need to be interspersed with sentences that use a variety of clause constructions. This will lend a musicality to the writing, and will allow for greater flow of language and ideas. Make sure to reread any written material to ensure that the syntax is correct and engaging. Otherwise, you may end up with something that comes off as confused rather than well-written.

Rewrite the following sentences by varying their syntax.

> Marilyn and Rosemary worked together. They were having a party. They had to get all the food done first. They cleaned the house and decorated. They invited about 20 people. The people were all work associates. They were having the party in Marilyn's backyard. This is where she had many similar parties. They were always fun.

This is one way to rewrite the sentences so that the syntax is varied:

Marilyn and Rosemary, who worked together, were going to have a party. But before they could do that, they had to get all the food ready for it, as well as clean the house and decorate. They invited about 20 people, who were all work associates, and were holding the party in Marilyn's backyard, where there had been many other parties that were always fun.

The rewritten sentences provide a greater variety of syntax, and consequently, greater rhythm. The language is more engaging as a result. Remember to make use of clauses to introduce information and create sentences that are complex. In addition, remember to reread any work you rewrite to make sure it makes sense.

Context clues

The term "context clues" refers to the words or phrases in the sentences that surround a new word or phrase. Context clues can often allow the reader to figure out the meaning of an unfamiliar word or phrase. Context clues may include examples of the new word or phrase, synonyms, antonyms, definitions, or contrasting information. By using context clues in the surrounding sentences, the reader can figure out approximately what the unknown word or phrase means. The placement of a word or a phrase is important, as is its function in a sentence. If a word or a phrase is being used as an adjective, the reader should look at the other adjectives in the sentence or the surrounding sentences to see if there is a clue to the word's or phrase's meaning. The location of a word or a phrase is also important. For instance, if a word or a phrase is at the beginning of a sentence, try to figure out its consequence; this may help the reader figure out its meaning.

Using context clues, determine the meaning of "fortuitous" as it is used in the following excerpt.

> Warren felt that meeting his nephew was quite <u>fortuitous,</u> since his nephew showed a real interest in getting involved in the company's business. Warren was hopeful that someday his nephew could take over for him.

To figure out the meaning of the word "fortuitous," the reader needs to analyze the rest of the sentence, as well as the following sentence. It would appear that their meeting was a good thing, since Warren was hopeful that his nephew could take over for him. The adjective "hopeful" helps the reader come to the conclusion that "fortuitous" means good or lucky. This is just one of the context clues. Another one would be that the nephew showed a real interest in his uncle's business. Always make sure to study the surrounding phrases and sentences for clues to an unknown word. The placement of the word or phrase and its function in the sentence are also important.

Explain how context clues can help the reader figure out the meaning of the phrase "prosthetic device" in the following excerpt.

> Modern artificial limbs are much better than artificial limbs of the past. These prosthetic devices have made it possible for amputees to run and to compete in sports. For instance, Vietnam veteran Bill Demby is able to play basketball in an aggressive, fast-paced, competitive manner thanks to high-tech plastic legs.

The placement of the phrase "prosthetic devices" helps the reader understand that the phrase is another way of saying "modern artificial limbs." This is the subject of the excerpt; the term "prosthetic devices" is a synonym for "modern artificial limbs." Even if the reader does not understand the meaning of "prosthetic," he or she can figure out the meaning of the expression. This shows how placement and context clues can assist a reader in learning the meaning of a word or an expression. Always study the information in an excerpt to better understand what is being said. The conclusion of the second sentence reinforces the meaning of the phrase by providing another synonym: "high-tech plastic legs."

How certain endings can indicate what part of speech a word is

The suffix of a word can be extremely important in telling a reader what function the word has in a sentence. Certain endings are used to make a stem an adjective; others are used to make a stem a noun. For instance, the root *consider* has many forms. It becomes a noun—*consideration*—with the addition of –*ation*. It becomes an adjective—*considerate*—with the addition of the suffix -*ate*. The adverb *considerately* can be made from the adjective *considerate* by adding *–ly*. This is a simple yet sophisticated method of figuring out what part of speech a word is.

The root word for *absolution* is *absolute*. The suffix *-tion* indicates that the word is a noun. The root could be combined with other suffixes to make other parts of speech as well. Add an *–ly* and you have the adverb *absolutely*. This word is a noun in its root form (*absolute*), so no change is needed to it. To make the verb *absolve*, the suffix *–ve* is added. This word is irregular, since most roots tend to be in verb form. It is important to be able to analyze a word, not just for its etymology, but also to determine what part of speech the word might be.

Discuss the etymology of the word fluctuate in the following sentence.

Tommy's mother noticed that his emotions tended to *fluctuate* a lot.

There really isn't a context clue in this statement, so you need to look up the word and discover its etymology to learn more about its meaning. The dictionary says that *fluctuate* is an intransitive verb, meaning it has no object. There are three syllables: fluc.tu.ate. The word has a Latin origin. It is derived from the verb "fluctuare," which means to undulate. You will also need to look up the word "undulate." It means to move in a wave-like motion, or to change continually. Synonyms of *fluctuate* are "alter," "shift," "swing," and "hesitate." In this usage, you can also see that there is a connotation of unpredictability. These clues give you a better understanding of the statement.

Using specialized reference materials to determine the pronunciation of a word

A print or digital dictionary can be used to find out many things about a word. A dictionary will show the correct pronunciation of a word, provide its meaning, and identify what part of speech the word is. It will also tell how the word was derived— that is, what words it came from originally. A dictionary will have a guide that shows how to sound out the words; it will use symbols to indicate sounds, and will also use sample sounds (the "a" in "bad," for instance). A dictionary lists all of the meanings of a word and the parts of speech the word can be used as. A thesaurus is useful because it lists synonyms for all the various meanings of a word, and it can help you clarify the precise meaning of a word as it is used in the text you are reading. This means you can find other words to use in a report or a text that mean the same thing as a word that may be used too often. Many books will have a glossary at the end to help you understand difficult or unfamiliar words used in the text.

Read the sentence below. Determine the meaning of "a partisan response."

> While at the meeting of the homeowners' association, Jeannie had the distinct feeling that there was a partisan response when all the other tenants belligerently shouted that they were just not going to accept any more increases in maintenance assessments, no matter what the condition of the roof was.

The meaning of the phrase can be determined from the context clues in the sentence. One big clue is the fact that the "other tenants belligerently shouted…" This suggests a tone of prejudice or unreasonableness. The sentence further suggests that there was something wrong with the roof that needed repairing, and that "no matter what," the other tenants were not willing to pay. Therefore, the reader can come to the conclusion that the phrase refers to a prejudiced reaction or response. If there were not enough clues in the sentence to determine the phrase's meaning, the word "partisan" could be looked up in a dictionary. Its meaning would explain the meaning of the phrase.

Analyze the following statement by Jesus Christ, which is found in the New Testament of the Bible.

> "If anyone comes to me and does not hate his own father and mother and wife and children and brothers and sisters, yes, and even his own life, he cannot be my disciple. And whoever does not carry their cross and follow me cannot be my disciple."(Luke 14:25-27)

This statement by Jesus that is quoted by Luke is an example of hyperbole. Hyperbole, or exaggeration to make a point, is frequently used throughout the Bible. It is not meant to be taken literally, and there is no command to hate family members or oneself. Rather, it is an entreaty that is meant to arouse intense emotion for maximum effect. The next sentence offers a clue in context for the reader's interpretation: one must be able to carry one's own cross (work hard) to be a disciple of Christ (i.e. to be a devout Christian). Therefore, the meaning is that devotion to God is more important than any relationship to any other family member, or any self-interest.

Nuances of "superfluous" and "outmoded"

Nuances are slight differences in the meanings of words that mean nearly the same thing. Nuances give words different tones or shades of meaning. They are similar to connotations, although usually more subtle. In the case of the words "superfluous" and "outmoded," superfluous conveys the sense that something is not and probably was never needed, while outmoded simply suggests that something is no longer of value since it is rendered needless due to age. Writers often use nuance to suggest something rather than saying it directly. This is often done through the choice of word or words that are used. Readers should always be aware of nuances, and should take them into account when considering the overall intent of a text.

Comprehension

It is important to acquire and accurately use words and phrases at the appropriate level to improve comprehension of various school subjects. Comprehension of academic and domain specific words is crucial to understanding the ideas and theories you will encounter as you move further in your academic career or enter the work force. Increased word knowledge that is domain specific helps individuals attain their academic and career goals. Therefore, it is very important to develop a system for increasing vocabulary through reading, using word lists, understanding word etymologies, and using new words in academic or work-related settings. A good vocabulary will result in greater personal achievements at a variety of levels.

Practice Test Part 1 Reading Comprehension

Practice Questions

Questions 1-10 refer to the following article:

Global warming and the depletion of natural resources are constant threats to the future of our planet. All people have a responsibility to be proactive participants in the fight to save Earth by working now to conserve resources for later. Participation begins with our everyday choices. From what you buy to what you do to how much you use, your decisions affect the planet and everyone around you. Now is the time to take action.

When choosing what to buy, look for **sustainable** products made from renewable or recycled resources. The packaging of the products you buy is just as important as the products themselves. Is the item minimally packaged in a recycled container? How did the product reach the store? Locally grown food and other products manufactured within your community are the best choices. The fewer miles a product traveled to reach you, the fewer resources it required.

You can continue to make a difference for the planet in how you use what you bought and the resources you have available. Remember the locally grown food you purchased? Don't pile it on your plate at dinner. Food that remains on your plate is a wasted resource, and you can always go back for seconds. You should try to be aware of your **consumption** of water and energy. Turn off the water when you brush your teeth, and limit your showers to five minutes. Turn off the lights, and don't leave appliances or chargers plugged in when not in use.

Together, we can use less, waste less, recycle more, and make the right choices. It may be the only chance we have.

1. What is the author's primary purpose in writing this article?

Ⓐ The author's purpose is to scare people.

Ⓑ The author's purpose is to warn people.

Ⓒ The author's purpose is to inspire people.

Ⓓ The author's purpose is to inform people.

This question has two parts. Answer Part A, then answer Part B.

2. Part A: How does the author make a connection between the second and third paragraphs?

Ⓐ The author indicates he will now make suggestions for how to use what you bought.

Ⓑ The author indicates he will continue to give more examples of what you should buy.

Ⓒ The author indicates he will make suggestions for how to keep from buying more items.

Ⓓ The author indicates he will make suggestions for how to tell other people what to buy.

Part B: What specific item is used as an example in paragraph 2 and 3?

Ⓐ Water

Ⓑ Food

Ⓒ Toys

Ⓓ Driving

3. What is the main idea of this article?

Ⓐ People should use less water and energy.

Ⓑ People should make responsible choices in what they purchase and how they use their available resources.

Ⓒ People are quickly destroying the earth, and there is no way to stop the destruction.

Ⓓ People should organize everyone they know to join the fight to save the environment.

4. Which organizational pattern did the author use?

Ⓐ Comparison and contrast

Ⓑ Chronological order

Ⓒ Cause and effect

Ⓓ Problem/solution

5. What does the author say is the place to begin saving our planet?

Ⓐ The place to begin is with getting rid of products that are not earth friendly.

Ⓑ The place to begin is with using less water when we take a shower.

Ⓒ The place to begin is with the choices we make every day.

Ⓓ The place to begin is with buying locally-grown food.

This question has two parts. Answer Part A, then answer Part B.
6. Part A: What does the author imply will happen if people do not follow his suggestions?

Ⓐ The author implies we will run out of resources in the next 10 years.

Ⓑ The author implies water and energy prices will rise sharply in the near future.

Ⓒ The author implies global warming and the depletion of natural resources will continue.

Ⓓ The author implies local farmers will lose their farms.

Part B: Which sentence supports your answer from Part A?

Ⓐ Food that remains on your plate is a wasted resource, and you can always go back for seconds.

Ⓑ From what you buy to what you do to how much you use, your decisions affect the planet and everyone around you.

Ⓒ Turn off the water when you brush your teeth, and limit your showers to five minutes.

Ⓓ Global warming and the depletion of natural resources are constant threats to the future of our planet.

7. You are working with a group to compile further research on what people can do to help the environment. Your teacher has asked your group to present a broad overview of the topic. Which of the following would be the best choice for dividing the topic among the individuals in your group?

Ⓐ Products that can be recycled, products that cannot be recycled, and products that should not be recycled.

Ⓑ Products that can be recycled, products that consume less energy, and products that use recycled packaging.

Ⓒ Products that can be recycled, hybrid cars, and water conservation.

Ⓓ Products that can be recycled, products that consume less energy, and accomplishing everyday tasks using environmentally friendly practices.

8. "When choosing what to buy, look for sustainable products made from renewable or recycled resources."
What does the word "sustainable" mean in the context of this selection?

Ⓐ Able to be maintained or kept in existence

Ⓑ Produced locally

Ⓒ Chosen for specific characteristics

Ⓓ Manufactured using an energy efficient process

This question has two parts. Answer Part A, then answer Part B.
9. Part A: "You should try to be aware of your consumption of water and energy."
What does the word "consumption" mean in the context of this selection?

Ⓐ Using the greatest amount

Ⓑ Illness of the lungs

Ⓒ Using the least amount

Ⓓ Depletion of goods

Part B: Based on your answer in Part A, give a sentence from the paragraph that supports your answer.

_____

_____

_____

10. The author makes a general suggestion to the reader: "You should try to be aware of your consumption of water and energy." Which of the following is one way the author specifies that this suggestion be carried out?

Ⓐ Food that remains on your plate is a wasted resource, and you can always go back for a second helping.

Ⓑ Locally grown food and other products manufactured within your community are the best choices.

Ⓒ Turn off the lights, and don't leave appliances or chargers plugged in when not in use.

Ⓓ Participation begins with our everyday choices.

Questions 11-19 refer to the following selection from Pride and Prejudice by Jane Austen:

It is a truth universally acknowledged, that a single man in possession of a good fortune, must be in want of a wife.

However little known the feelings or views of such a man may be on his first entering a neighbourhood, this truth is so well fixed in the minds of the surrounding families, that he is considered the rightful property of some one or other of their daughters.

"My dear Mr. Bennet," said his lady to him one day, "have you heard that Netherfield Park is let at last?"

Mr. Bennet replied that he had not.

"But it is," returned she; "for Mrs. Long has just been here, and she told me all about it."

Mr. Bennet made no answer.

"Do you not want to know who has taken it?" cried his wife impatiently.

"You want to tell me, and I have no objection to hearing it."

This was invitation enough.

"Why, my dear, you must know, Mrs. Long says that Netherfield is taken by a young man of large fortune from the north of England; that he came down on Monday in a chaise and four to see the place, and was so much delighted with it, that he agreed with Mr. Morris immediately; that he is to take possession before Michaelmas, and some of his servants are to be in the house by the end of next week."

"What is his name?"

"Bingley."

"Is he married or single?"

"Oh! Single, my dear, to be sure! A single man of large fortune; four or five thousand a year. What a fine thing for our girls!"

"How so? How can it affect them?"

"My dear Mr. Bennet," replied his wife, "how can you be so tiresome!" You must know that I am thinking of his marrying one of them."

"Is that his design in settling here?"

"Design! Nonsense, how can you talk so! But it is very likely that he may fall in love with one of them, and therefore you must visit him as soon as he comes."

"I see no occasion for that. You and the girls may go, or you may send them by themselves, which perhaps will be still better, for as you are as handsome as any of them, Mr. Bingley may like you the best of the party."

11. What is the central idea of this selection?

Ⓐ A new neighbor is due to arrive who may become good friends with Mr. and Mrs. Bennet.

Ⓑ A new neighbor is due to arrive who may be a prospective husband for one of the Bennet daughters.

Ⓒ A new neighbor is due to arrive who may be a good business connection for Mr. Bennet.

Ⓓ A new neighbor is due to arrive who has already expressed an interest in marrying one of the Bennet daughters.

12. How does Mrs. Bennet feel about the arrival of Mr. Bingley?

Ⓐ Mrs. Bennet is excited about the arrival of Mr. Bingley.

Ⓑ Mrs. Bennet is nervous about the arrival of Mr. Bingley.

Ⓒ Mrs. Bennet is afraid the arrival of Mr. Bingley will upset Mr. Bennet.

Ⓓ Mrs. Bennet is indifferent to the arrival of Mr. Bingley.

13. What does Mrs. Bennet expect from Mr. Bennet?

Ⓐ Mrs. Bennet expects Mr. Bennet to invite Mr. Bingley to a dinner party.

Ⓑ Mrs. Bennet expects Mr. Bennet to offer one of his daughters in marriage to Mr. Bingley.

Ⓒ Mrs. Bennet expects Mr. Bennet to pay a visit to Mr. Bingley.

Ⓓ Mrs. Bennet expects Mr. Bennet to invite Mr. Bingley to a ball in his honor.

14. What does Mrs. Bennet expect from Mr. Bingley?

Ⓐ Mrs. Bennet expects Mr. Bingley to be interested in marrying one of her daughters.

Ⓑ Mrs. Bennet expects Mr. Bingley to be interested in receiving a visit from Mr. Bennet.

Ⓒ Mrs. Bennet expects Mr. Bingley to love living at Netherfield Park.

Ⓓ Mrs. Bennet expects Mr. Bingley to ask for her help in choosing a wife for himself.

This question has two parts. Answer Part A, then answer Part B.
15. Part A: Which of the following statements best describes Mrs. Bennet's feelings about her husband as indicated by this selection?

Ⓐ Mrs. Bennet is tired of her husband.

Ⓑ Mrs. Bennet is exasperated by her husband.

Ⓒ Mrs. Bennet is afraid of her husband.

Ⓓ Mrs. Bennet is indifferent toward her husband.

Part B: Which sentence form the story lets you know that she feels this way?

Ⓐ Mr. Bennet thinks his wife is a great beauty.

Ⓑ "What is his name?"

Ⓒ "My dear Mr. Bennet," replied his wife, "how can you be so tiresome!"

Ⓓ "My dear Mr. Bennet," said his lady to him one day, "have you heard that Netherfield Park is let at last?"

16. This selection is set in England at the beginning of the 19th century. Drawing on information from this selection, what could you conclude was a primary goal for young women in England during this time period?

Ⓐ To marry

Ⓑ To marry a man with money

Ⓒ To entertain the neighbors

Ⓓ To be courted by as many men as possible

17. "<u>It is a truth universally acknowledged</u>, that a single man in possession of a good fortune, must be in want of a wife."
Which of the following most nearly matches the meaning of the underlined phrase?

    Ⓐ Everyone knows

    Ⓑ The universe has decided

    Ⓒ It is a documented fact

    Ⓓ It is best to tell the truth

18. "It is a truth universally acknowledged, <u>that a single man in possession of a good fortune, must be in want of a wife.</u>"
Which of the following most nearly matches the meaning of the underlined phrase?

    Ⓐ An unmarried man always wants to get married.

    Ⓑ An unmarried man must want to give his money away.

    Ⓒ An unmarried man with money always wants to get married.

    Ⓓ An unmarried man can increase his fortune by getting married.

19. "**Is that his design in settling here?**"
What does the word **design** mean in the context of this selection?

    Ⓐ Intention

    Ⓑ Drawing

    Ⓒ Creation

    Ⓓ Improvisation

Questions 20 -24 pertain to the following passage:

Caged

(1) I am caged.
(2) Dim, dark, dank,
(3) Depressing metal bars
(4) Are my home,
(5) My window on the world.
(6) But for one hour each day—
(7) Sixty precious, priceless minutes—
(8) I am led from the dungeon
(9) Into the bright, blinding light.
(10) That is my sanctuary,
(11) Wrapped in chain link
(12) And barbed wire.
(13) The air is sweeter,
(14) Tinged with freedom
(15) And fragranced with memories
(16) Of a lifetime so long ago
(17) It has almost been forgotten.
(18) I bathe in the welcome warmth,
(19) Cleanse my soul in the newborn breeze.
(20) I confess my sins
(21) In the brazen light of day,
(22) And hope springs eternal once again.
(23) But then they come.
(24) My time is up.
(25) Another hour of life has expired.
(26) And I return to the depths
(27) Of despair, discouragement, defeat.
(28) Freedom, forgiveness, and faith are forgotten.
(29) I am caged.

20. What is the connotation of the word "dungeon" in line 8?

Ⓐ The narrator lives in the basement of a castle

Ⓑ This poem is set in medieval times

Ⓒ The narrator's life is dark and unrelenting

Ⓓ The narrator is uncomfortable with life

21. What is the setting for this poem?

Ⓐ A prison

Ⓑ A farm

Ⓒ A house

Ⓓ A school

This question has two parts. Answer Part A, then answer Part B.

22. Part A: Which literary device is used throughout this poem to underscore the repetitive nature of the narrator's life?

Ⓐ Simile

Ⓑ Paradox

Ⓒ Onomatopoeia

Ⓓ Alliteration

Part B: Give an example of this literary device from the story.

_____

_____

_____

23. What point of view is used in this poem?

Ⓐ First person

Ⓑ Second person

Ⓒ Third person

Ⓓ All of the above

24. What do lines 18-22 reference?

Ⓐ The narrator's love of sunny days

Ⓑ The narrator's desire for a fresh start

Ⓒ The narrator's anger at the circumstances

Ⓓ The narrator's memories of a normal life

Answers and Explanations

1. D: Various parts of the article are intended to scare (choice A), warn (choice B), and inspire (choice C) people, but the primary purpose of the article is to offer practical advice about what products people should buy and how to use their available resources to make responsible decisions for the future of our planet.

2. Part A: A: The author begins the third paragraph with, "You can continue to make a difference for the planet in how you use what you bought and the resources you have available." This sentence makes the connection between the second paragraph which deals with what people should buy and the third paragraph which makes suggestions for how to use what they have.

Part B: B: In paragraph 2 he mentions "Locally grown food and other products," and in paragraph 3 he mentions "Remember the locally grown food you purchased?"

3. B: The author does suggest that people should use less water and energy (choice A), but these are only two suggestions among many and not the main idea of the article. The article does not say that people are destroying the earth (choice C) or make a suggestion that people organize their acquaintances (choice D).

4. D: The author presents the problems of global warming and the rapid depletion of the planet's natural resources and offers several practical suggestions for how to stop global warming and use remaining resources judiciously.

5. C: The author makes suggestions to use less water (choice B) and buy locally grown food (choice D), but they are not suggested as the place to begin saving the planet. The author does not suggest getting rid of products that are not earth friendly (choice A). The author states: "Participation begins with our everyday choices."

6. Part A: C: The author does not mention running out of resources in a specific time period (choice A), the cost of water and energy (choice B), or the possibility of hardship for local farmers (choice D).

Part B: D: The sentence that best shows that the author is implying that global warming and the depletion of natural resources will continue is, "Global warming and the depletion of natural resources are constant threats to the future of our planet."

7. D: Choice D gives the broadest interpretation of the topic. Choice A focuses solely on recycling; choice B focuses on the choice of products to be purchased; and choice C focuses on recycling, one type of energy-saving product (hybrid cars), and ways to conserve one resource (water).

8. A: "When choosing what to buy, look for sustainable products made from renewable or recycled resources." The context of this sentence indicates that sustainable means renewable or able to be used again.

9. Part A: D: As the passage states: "You should try to be aware of your consumption of water and energy. Turn off the water when you brush your teeth, and limit your showers to five minutes. Turn off the lights, and don't leave appliances or chargers plugged in when not in use." The contexts of these sentences indicate that consumption means the depletion of goods (e.g., water and energy).

Part B: Any of the sentences above that give context to what the word "consumption" mean are acceptable answers.

10. C: Of the choices available, this is the only sentence that offers specific ideas for carrying out the author's suggestion to the reader of limiting consumption of energy.

11. B: There is no indication in the passage that the Bennets are interested in becoming friends with Mr. Bingley (choice A), that Mr. Bingley would be a valuable business connection (choice C), or that Mr. Bingley has any prior knowledge of the Bennet daughters (choice D). Mrs. Bennet tells her husband that a new neighbor is moving in: "Mrs. Long says that Netherfield is taken by a young man of large fortune." Mrs. Bennet is sure he will make an excellent husband for one of her daughters: "You must know that I am thinking of his marrying one of them."

12. A: Mrs. Bennet feels that Mr. Bingley is likely to marry one of her daughters. She tells her husband that Mr. Bingley is a "single man of large fortune; four or five thousand a year. What a fine thing for our girls!"

13. C: Mrs. Bennet wants her husband to be acquainted with Mr. Bingley so that he can introduce Mr. Bingley to their daughters: "But it is very likely that he may fall in love with one of them, and therefore you must visit him as soon as he comes."

14. A: Mrs. Bennet remarks to her husband, "But it is very likely that he may fall in love with one of them, and therefore you must visit him as soon as he comes."

15. Part A: B: Mrs. Bennet is annoyed and fed up with her husband's seeming indifference to Mr. Bingley: "'My dear Mr. Bennet,' replied his wife, 'how can you be so tiresome!'"

Part B: C: This sentence best represents how she feels about her husband.

16. B: The evidence in this selection indicates that marrying a man with money was a primary goal for young women. Mrs. Bennet tells Mr. Bennet that Mr. Bingley is "A single man of large fortune; four or five thousand a year." Mrs. Bennet further indicates that she is thrilled with the news because of Mr. Bingley's potential as a husband for one of her daughters: "What a fine thing for our girls... You must know that I am thinking of his marrying one of them."

17. A: "It is a truth universally acknowledged" means that something is understood to be true by the general public.

18. C: "A single man in possession of a good fortune, must be in want of a wife" means that if a man has enough money to support a wife in comfort, he must want to find a wife as soon as possible.

19. A: Mr. Bennet is facetiously asking if the idea of marriage (particularly to one of his own daughters) was Mr. Bingley's intention when he agreed to rent Netherfield Park.

20. C: is the best choice because the connotation of the word "dungeon" is that the narrator's life is dark and unrelenting. A, B, and D are not the best choices because they do not accurately represent the real connotation of the word "dungeon."

21. A: is the best choice because "Caged" is set in a prison, as can be deduced from careful reading. B, C, and D are not the best choices because the poem is not set on a farm or in a house or school.

22. Part A: D: is the best choice because alliteration is used throughout the poem to underscore the repetitive nature of the narrator's life. A, B, and C are not the best choices because simile, paradox, and onomatopoeia are not used throughout this poem.

Part B: There are several examples that can be used here. Two of them are, "Dim, dark, dank" and "bright, blinding light".

23. A: is the best choice because this poem is written using first-person point of view. B and C are not the best choices because this poem is not written using second-person or third-person point of view. D is not the best choice because the poem is only written in first-person point of view.

24. B: is the best choice because lines 18-22 reference the narrator's desire for a fresh start. A, C, and D are not the best choices because they do not accurately reflect the theme of lines 18-22.

Practice Test Part 2 Writing From Sources: Argument

Directions: Closely read each of the four texts provided below and write an evidence-based argument on the topic below. You may use the margins to take notes as you read and the space to plan your response. Write your response in the space provided at the end of the four texts.

Topic: Should the United States still be on the gold standard?

Your Task: Carefully read each of the four texts provided. Then, using evidence from at least two of the texts, write a well-developed argument regarding whether or not the U.S. should still be on the gold standard. Clearly establish your claim, distinguish your claim from alternate or opposing claims, and use specific and relevant evidence from at least two of the texts to develop your argument. Do not simply summarize each text.

Text 1

Abandoning the gold standard was a seminal moment, and one we're now all paying for

(1) On 15 August 1971, with the US public finances straitened by the cost of the war in Vietnam, Richard Nixon finally cut the link between the US dollar and gold. Until then, the US Treasury was duty bound to exchange an ounce of gold with central banks willing to pay them $35.

(2) Suddenly, for the first time in history, the level of the world's currencies depended not on the value of gold or some other tangible commodity but on the amount of trust investors had in that currency. Central banks were allowed to set monetary policy based on their instincts rather than on the need to keep their currency in line with gold.

(3) It was one of those seminal moments whose significance has only gradually become apparent, obscured as it was at the time by Vietnam and then Watergate. But the more one examines economic history, the more obvious it is that this was one of the most important policy decisions in modern history.

(4) Let's start with first principles: for as long as anyone can remember, politicians have sought to spend more than they can afford. Since the invention of money they have discovered ever more ingenious ways to do so.

(5) The initial method involved debasing the currency. Henry VIII earned his nickname "Old Coppernose" because he added so much copper to what were supposed to be silver coins that eventually it would show through on the nose of his portrait.

These bouts of debasement typically end in disaster, as faith is lost in the currency, inflation shoots through the roof and the economy collapses, after which politicians introduce a new, more credible system.

(6) After trust evaporated in gold and silver coinage, we had the gold standard and then the Bretton Woods system and now, today, fiat money – but the routine is painfully familiar. The main difference with fiat money is that whereas under the gold standard it was all too obvious when politicians were spending beyond their means (they would simply run out of gold reserves), these days it is slightly more difficult to tell quite how close the system is to breakage.

(7) Nonetheless, as we look back at the chaos of the past few weeks, it is quite clear that our current version is on its last legs. This, in essence, was the point Sir Mervyn King tried to make again and again in the Inflation Report press conference last

week: 2008 was only one stage in a far bigger crisis of confidence in the way we have structured the world economy.

(8) Over the past 40 years, in the absence of a coherent international monetary system and under the veil of floating currencies, countries which would otherwise have been penalised for doing so were allowed to borrow enormous amounts (eg. The US and UK, or Greece). Other countries (eg. China or Germany) indulged them by lending enormous amounts. In the meantime, investors convinced themselves that the apparent economic growth fuelled by this debt was genuine rather than an artificial product of a binge.

(9) No doubt gold is in a bubble, but all bubbles start with the germ of a good idea, which in this case is that the present system for running the world economy is close to breakage. It would be nice to believe that policymakers could ferret their way out of their current pickle without further debauching their currencies, but, politically at least, that is always the easy way out.

(10) Unfortunately, currency debasement is a competitive sort of thing, as countries vie to reduce the value of their money (and hence their debt). There has been some talk of "currency war" in recent years, but this is nothing in comparison with the competitive devaluation and protectionism in the 1930s as the inter-war gold standard came to an end. However, the precedent is ominous.

(11) As ever these days, any hope, such as it is, lies in China. It is fast realising that its investment in US debt will not be fully repaid.

(12) However, in the long run it has two options: to allow the US to debase or default; or to negotiate, forgive a chunk of the debt and dramatically reduce those imbalances. ...

--- Edmund Conway
Excerpted from http://www.telegraph.co.uk, August 13, 2011

Text 2

Why Do People Want A Gold Standard When History Shows Us It Does Not Last?

(1) It is curious to me that so many libertarians are dead set against any form of currency other than gold when history has made it abundantly clear that a gold standard cannot be maintained.

(2) Consider that as soon as gold is represented by paper (or digital account balances), all the checks against inflation of the money supply that gold provides are lost. In order to argue that gold cannot be inflated, one must also argue that all transactions in the economy must take place using physical specie.

(3) Clearly this presents a problem in our digital age. Imagine trying to buy something from Amazon.com. You would have to place an order, and then mail your gold bullion to the seller. There could literally be no digital accounts of gold at all if one wanted to ensure that the money supply could never be co-opted and inflated. Obviously this would require the imposition of State rules to prevent people from digitally representing gold for its use as a money.

(4) Clearly in order for gold to function as a currency in our modern age, it *must* be represented either by paper or digital account. Which means it is ultimately of no more use in preventing inflation than if the government simply created rules today outlawing the inflation of dollars.

(5) I argue that what "backs money" is unimportant. What matters is that the units of account that people use cannot be inflated. What matters is that I cannot simply alter an account balance by plugging some numbers into a computer.

(6) Fortunately for us today, such a currency exists. It is called Bitcoin. It is a decentralized peer-to-peer encrypted currency system that totally prevents arbitrary inflation of the units of account. With bitcoins, one cannot simply increase an account balance of Bitcoins by arbitrarily entering some numbers into a computer. The actual currency itself is unreproducible.

(7) In order to increase a Bitcoin account balance, the transaction must be validated against the entire peer-to-peer network. The entire network knows the account balance of every wallet in existence and it will refuse any changes that attempt to alter number of Bitcoins in existence. Bitcoin account balances simply cannot be inflated. ...

--- Michael Suede
Excerpted from https://www.libertariannews.org, December 1, 2011

Text 3

Back to the gold standard? It makes no economic sense

(1) Ever since Richard Nixon ended the convertibility of the US dollar into gold in 1971, there have been calls for a return to some form of gold standard. Proponents of this view, often known as "gold bugs", want to see an end to paper money guaranteed by promises and for currencies to once more be backed by precious metal. In the last few years as central banks around the world have engaged in quantitative easing to try and support their economies these voices have become louder. Monday night's Analysis on Radio 4 looked at the argument in some detail.

(2) The specific appeal of gold can be hard to rationalise: it might be aesthetically pleasing, but does that make it a sound basis for a monetary system? Sometimes I wonder if gold bugs just listened to too much Spandau Ballet in the 1980s. In the programme, Robert Skidelsky argued that supporters of the gold standard have an almost atavistic belief in its powers, rooted in the age-old worship of sun gods.

(3)What they tend to ignore is that the world has tried the gold standard before and it was, in most respects, a disaster. At present, as the economy grows and produces more goods the central bank can expand the money supply to keep up with output. Under the gold standard, as output increases, the money supply will be fixed and with more goods but the same amount of money, prices will tend to fall.

(4)Falling prices might sound like a good thing, and in individual cases they often are, but a falling general price level is usually associated with severe economic strains. Why buy anything today if it will be cheaper next week? The end result tends to be falling output, rising unemployment, falling wages and a large increase in the real burden of debt. ...

--- Duncan Weldon
Excerpted from http://www.theguardian.com, July 3, 2012

Text 4

Why the U.S. Should Return to the Gold Standard – Even Though it Won't

(1) Many analysts fear that the Fed's policy of pouring $2.3 trillion into the economy in an attempt to spur growth is really only fostering inflation and devaluing the dollar – with potentially disastrous consequences. Fixing the value of the dollar to gold would mean more money could not be printed unless more gold was obtained to back it up. Historically, economies using a gold standard currency enjoy stable prices – governments can't print the excess money that causes inflation – and governments without excess money can't spend themselves into massive debt. That's why many local activists and legislatures are pushing for a return to the gold standard.

(2)Social conservative group American Principles in Action joined forces with the Iowa Tea Party in June to set up a "Gold Standard 2012" bus tour that included appearances by several Republican presidential contenders.
Also last month, three Republican senators introduced a bill to Congress, the Sound Money Promotion Act, which would make it easier to use gold and silver coins as currency. Utah has gone even further – its Legal Tender Act of 2011 makes it possible to use gold and silver as cash, but with the value based on weight.

(3)"Fiat currencies are frequently manipulated in such a way to finance the large-scale expansion of national governments," Sen. Mike Lee, R-UT, told *Smart Money*. "The expanded discussion about the need for at least the option of precious metal currency systems is because of that fear."
The world went off the gold standard in 1914 because the powers of Europe needed to print more money than the gold standard would allow in order to pay for World War I.

(4) The gold standard reappeared just after World War II as part of the Bretton Woods agreement. The idea was to avoid the international monetary chaos of the interwar period, particularly the Great Depression, by tying currency to gold. Unfortunately, only the U.S. dollar was actually convertible to gold; other currencies were pegged to the dollar. The system relied upon the U.S. government acting in a fiscally responsible manner. ...

--- David Zeiler
Excerpted from http://www.theguardian.com, July 12, 2011

Practice Test Part 3 Text-Analysis Response

Your Task: Closely read the text provided on the following pages and write a well-developed, text-based response of two to three paragraphs. In your response, identify a central idea in the text and analyze how the author's use of one writing strategy (literary element or literary technique or rhetorical device) develops this central idea. Use strong and thorough evidence from the text to support your analysis. Do not simply summarize the text. You may use the margins to take notes as you read and scrap paper to plan your response. Write your response in the space provided on the page that follows the text.

Guidelines:

Be sure to

• Identify a central idea in the text
• Analyze how the author's use of one writing strategy (literary element or literary technique or rhetorical device) develops this central idea. Examples include: characterization, conflict, denotation/connotation, metaphor, simile, irony, language use, point-of-view, setting, structure, symbolism, theme, tone, etc.
• Use strong and thorough evidence from the text to support your analysis
• Organize your ideas in a cohesive and coherent manner
• Maintain a formal style of writing
• Follow the conventions of standard written English

The Story of My Life
By Helen Keller

THE most important day I remember in all my life is the one on which my teacher, Anne Mansfield Sullivan, came to me. I am filled with wonder when I consider the immeasurable contrasts between the two lives which it connects. It was the third of March, 1887, three months before I was seven years old.

On the afternoon of that eventful day, I stood on the porch, dumb, expectant. I guessed vaguely from my mother's signs and from the hurrying to and fro in the house that something unusual was about to happen, so I went to the door and waited on the steps. The afternoon sun penetrated the mass of honeysuckle that covered the porch, and fell on my upturned face. My fingers lingered almost unconsciously on the familiar leaves and blossoms which had just come forth to greet the sweet southern spring. I did not know what the future held of marvel or surprise for me. Anger and bitterness had preyed upon me continually for weeks and a deep languor had succeeded this passionate struggle.

Have you ever been at sea in a dense fog, when it seemed as if a tangible white darkness shut you in, and the great ship, tense and anxious, groped her way toward the shore with plummet and sounding-line, and you waited with beating heart for something to happen? I was like that ship before my education began, only I was without compass or sounding-line, and had no way of knowing how near the harbour was. "Light! give me light!" was the wordless cry of my soul, and the light of love shone on me in that very hour.

I felt approaching footsteps. I stretched out my hand as I supposed to my mother. Someone took it, and I was caught up and held close in the arms of her who had come to reveal all things to me, and, more than all things else, to love me.

The morning after my teacher came she led me into her room and gave me a doll. The little blind children at the Perkins Institution had sent it and Laura Bridgman had dressed it; but I did not know this until afterward. When I had played with it a little while, Miss Sullivan slowly spelled into my hand the word "d-o-l-l." I was at once interested in this finger play and tried to imitate it. When I finally succeeded in making the letters correctly I was flushed with childish pleasure and pride. Running downstairs to my mother I held up my hand and made the letters for doll. I did not know that I was spelling a word or even that words existed; I was simply making my fingers go in monkey-like imitation. In the days that followed I learned to spell in this uncomprehending way a great many words, among them *pin, hat, cup* and a few verbs like *sit, stand* and *walk.* But my teacher had been with me several weeks before I understood that everything has a name.

One day, while I was playing with my new doll, Miss Sullivan put my big rag doll into my lap also, spelled "d-o-l-l" and tried to make me understand that "d-o-l-l" applied to both. Earlier in the day we had had a tussle over the words "m-u-g" and "w-a-t-e-r." Miss Sullivan had tried to impress it upon me that "m-u-g" is *mug* and that "w-a-t-e-r" is *water*, but I persisted in confounding the two. In despair she had dropped the subject for the time, only to renew it at the first opportunity. I became impatient at her repeated attempts and, seizing the new doll, I dashed it upon the floor. I was keenly delighted when I felt the fragments of the broken doll at my feet. Neither sorrow nor regret followed my passionate outburst. I had not loved the doll. In the still, dark world in which I lived there was no strong sentiment of tenderness. I felt my teacher sweep the fragments to one side of the hearth, and I had a sense of satisfaction that the cause of my discomfort was removed. She brought me my hat, and I knew I was going out into the warm sunshine. This thought, if a wordless sensation may be called a thought, made me hop and skip with pleasure.

We walked down the path to the well-house, attracted by the fragrance of the honeysuckle with which it was covered. Someone was drawing water and my teacher placed my hand under the spout. As the cool stream gushed over one hand she spelled into the other the word water, first slowly, then rapidly. I stood still, my whole attention fixed upon the motions of her fingers. Suddenly I felt a misty consciousness as of something forgotten–a thrill of returning thought; and somehow the mystery of language was revealed to me. I knew then that "w-a-t-e-r" meant the wonderful cool something that was flowing over my hand. That living word awakened my soul, gave it light, hope, joy, set it free! There were barriers still, it is true, but barriers that could in time be swept away.

I left the well-house eager to learn. Everything had a name, and each name gave birth to a new thought. As we returned to the house every object which I touched seemed to quiver with life. That was because I saw everything with the strange, new sight that had come to me. On entering the door I remembered the doll I had broken. I felt my way to the hearth and picked up the pieces. I tried vainly to put them together. Then my eyes filled with tears; for I realized what I had done, and for the first time I felt repentance and sorrow.

I learned a great many new words that day. I do not remember what they all were; but I do know that *mother, father, sister, teacher* were among them–words that were to make the world blossom for me, "like Aaron's rod, with flowers." It would have been difficult to find a happier child than I was as I lay in my crib at the close of the eventful day and lived over the joys it had brought me, and for the first time longed for a new day to come.

I RECALL many incidents of the summer of 1887 that followed my soul's sudden awakening. I did nothing but explore with my hands and learn the name of every object that I touched; and the more I handled things and learned their names and uses, the more joyous and confident grew my sense of kinship with the rest of the world.

When the time of daisies and buttercups came Miss Sullivan took me by the hand across the fields, where men were preparing the earth for the seed, to the banks of the Tennessee River, and there, sitting on the warm grass, I had my first lessons in the beneficence of nature. I learned how the sun and the rain make to grow out of the ground every tree that is pleasant to the sight and good for food, how birds build their nests and live and thrive from land to land, how the squirrel, the deer, the lion and every other creature finds food and shelter. As my knowledge of things grew I felt more and more the delight of the world I was in. Long before I learned to do a sum in arithmetic or describe the shape of the earth, Miss Sullivan had taught me to find beauty in the fragrant woods, in every blade of grass, and in the curves and dimples of my baby sister's hand. She linked my earliest thoughts with nature, and made me feel that "birds and flowers and I were happy peers."

But about this time I had an experience which taught me that nature is not always kind. One day my teacher and I were returning from a long ramble. The morning had been fine, but it was growing warm and sultry when at last we turned our faces homeward. Two or three times we stopped to rest under a tree by the wayside. Our last halt was under a wild cherry tree a short distance from the house. The shade was grateful, and the tree was so easy to climb that with my teacher's assistance I was able to scramble to a seat in the branches. It was so cool up in the tree that Miss Sullivan proposed that we have our luncheon there. I promised to keep still while she went to the house to fetch it.

Suddenly a change passed over the tree. All the sun's warmth left the air. I knew the sky was black, because all the heat, which meant light to me, had died out of the atmosphere. A strange odour came up from the earth. I knew it, it was the odour that always precedes a thunderstorm, and a nameless fear clutched at my heart. I felt absolutely alone, cut off from my friends and the firm earth. The immense, the unknown, enfolded me. I remained still and expectant; a chilling terror crept over me. I longed for my teacher's return; but above all things I wanted to get down from that tree.

There was a moment of sinister silence, then a multitudinous stirring of the leaves. A shiver ran through the tree, and the wind sent forth a blast that would have knocked me off had I not clung to the branch with might and main. The tree swayed and strained. The small twigs snapped and fell about me in showers. A wild impulse to jump seized me, but terror held me fast. I crouched down in the fork of the tree. The branches lashed about me. I felt the intermittent jarring that came now and then, as if something heavy had fallen and the shock had traveled up till it reached the limb I sat on. It worked my suspense up to the highest point, and just as I was thinking the tree and I should fall together, my teacher seized my hand and helped me down. I clung to her, trembling with joy to feel the earth under my feet once more. I had learned a new lesson–that nature "wages open war against her children, and under softest touch hides treacherous claws."

Success Strategies

The most important thing you can do is to ignore your fears and jump into the test immediately. Do not be overwhelmed by any strange-sounding terms. You have to jump into the test like jumping into a pool—all at once is the easiest way.

Make Predictions

As you read and understand the question, try to guess what the answer will be. Remember that several of the answer choices are wrong, and once you begin reading them, your mind will immediately become cluttered with answer choices designed to throw you off. Your mind is typically the most focused immediately after you have read the question and digested its contents. If you can, try to predict what the correct answer will be. You may be surprised at what you can predict.

Quickly scan the choices and see if your prediction is in the listed answer choices. If it is, then you can be quite confident that you have the right answer. It still won't hurt to check the other answer choices, but most of the time, you've got it!

Answer the Question

It may seem obvious to only pick answer choices that answer the question, but the test writers can create some excellent answer choices that are wrong. Don't pick an answer just because it sounds right, or you believe it to be true. It MUST answer the question. Once you've made your selection, always go back and check it against the question and make sure that you didn't misread the question and that the answer choice does answer the question posed.

Benchmark

After you read the first answer choice, decide if you think it sounds correct or not. If it doesn't, move on to the next answer choice. If it does, mentally mark that answer choice. This doesn't mean that you've definitely selected it as your answer choice, it just means that it's the best you've seen thus far. Go ahead and read the next choice. If the next choice is worse than the one you've already selected, keep going to the next answer choice. If the next choice is better than the choice you've already selected, mentally mark the new answer choice as your best guess.

The first answer choice that you select becomes your standard. Every other answer choice must be benchmarked against that standard. That choice is correct until proven otherwise by another answer choice beating it out. Once you've decided that no other answer choice seems as good, do one final check to ensure that your answer choice answers the question posed.

Valid Information

Don't discount any of the information provided in the question. Every piece of information may be necessary to determine the correct answer. None of the information in the question is there to throw you off (while the answer choices will certainly have information to throw you off). If two seemingly unrelated topics are discussed, don't ignore either. You can be confident there is a relationship, or it wouldn't be included in the question, and you are probably going to have to determine what is that relationship to find the answer.

Avoid "Fact Traps"

Don't get distracted by a choice that is factually true. Your search is for the answer that answers the question. Stay focused and don't fall for an answer that is true but irrelevant. Always go back to the question and make sure you're choosing an answer that actually answers the question and is not just a true statement. An answer can be factually correct, but it MUST answer the question asked. Additionally, two answers can both be seemingly correct, so be sure to read all of the answer choices, and make sure that you get the one that BEST answers the question.

Milk the Question

Some of the questions may throw you completely off. They might deal with a subject you have not been exposed to, or one that you haven't reviewed in years. While your lack of knowledge about the subject will be a hindrance, the question itself can give you many clues that will help you find the correct answer. Read the question carefully and look for clues. Watch particularly for adjectives and nouns describing difficult terms or words that you don't recognize. Regardless of whether you completely understand a word or not, replacing it with a synonym, either provided or one you more familiar with, may help you to understand what the questions are asking. Rather than wracking your mind about specific detailed information concerning a difficult term or word, try to use mental substitutes that are easier to understand.

The Trap of Familiarity

Don't just choose a word because you recognize it. On difficult questions, you may not recognize a number of words in the answer choices. The test writers don't put "make-believe" words on the test, so don't think that just because you only recognize all the words in one answer choice that that answer choice must be correct. If you only recognize words in one answer choice, then focus on that one. Is it correct? Try your best to determine if it is correct. If it is, that's great. If not, eliminate it. Each word and answer choice you eliminate increases your chances of getting the question correct, even if you then have to guess among the unfamiliar choices.

Eliminate Answers

Eliminate choices as soon as you realize they are wrong. But be careful! Make sure you consider all of the possible answer choices. Just because one appears right, doesn't mean that the next one won't be even better! The test writers will usually put more than one good answer choice for every question, so read all of them. Don't worry if you are stuck between two that seem right. By getting down to just two remaining possible choices, your odds are now 50/50. Rather than wasting too much time, play the odds. You are guessing, but guessing wisely because you've been able to knock out some of the answer choices that you know are wrong. If you are eliminating choices and realize that the last answer choice you are left with is also obviously wrong, don't panic. Start over and consider each choice again. There may easily be something that you missed the first time and will realize on the second pass.

Tough Questions

If you are stumped on a problem or it appears too hard or too difficult, don't waste time. Move on! Remember though, if you can quickly check for obviously incorrect answer choices, your chances of guessing correctly are greatly improved. Before you completely give up, at least try to knock out a couple of possible answers. Eliminate what you can and then guess at the remaining answer choices before moving on.

Brainstorm

If you get stuck on a difficult question, spend a few seconds quickly brainstorming. Run through the complete list of possible answer choices. Look at each choice and ask yourself, "Could this answer the question satisfactorily?" Go through each answer choice and consider it independently of the others. By systematically going through all possibilities, you may find something that you would otherwise overlook. Remember though that when you get stuck, it's important to try to keep moving.

Read Carefully

Understand the problem. Read the question and answer choices carefully. Don't miss the question because you misread the terms. You have plenty of time to read each question thoroughly and make sure you understand what is being asked. Yet a happy medium must be attained, so don't waste too much time. You must read carefully, but efficiently.

Face Value

When in doubt, use common sense. Always accept the situation in the problem at face value. Don't read too much into it. These problems will not require you to make huge leaps of logic. The test writers aren't trying to throw you off with a cheap trick. If you have to go beyond creativity and make a leap of logic in order to have an answer choice answer the question, then you should look at the other answer choices. Don't overcomplicate the problem by creating theoretical relationships or explanations that will warp time or space. These are normal problems rooted in reality. It's just that the applicable relationship or explanation may not be readily apparent and you have to figure things out. Use your common sense to interpret anything that isn't clear.

Prefixes

If you're having trouble with a word in the question or answer choices, try dissecting it. Take advantage of every clue that the word might include. Prefixes and suffixes can be a huge help. Usually they allow you to determine a basic meaning. Pre- means before, post- means after, pro - is positive, de- is negative. From these prefixes and suffixes, you can get an idea of the general meaning of the word and try to put it into context. Beware though of any traps. Just because con- is the opposite of pro-, doesn't necessarily mean congress is the opposite of progress!

Hedge Phrases

Watch out for critical hedge phrases, led off with words such as "likely," "may," "can," "sometimes," "often," "almost," "mostly," "usually," "generally," "rarely," and "sometimes." Question writers insert these hedge phrases to cover every possibility. Often an answer choice will be wrong simply because it leaves no room for exception. Unless the situation calls for them, avoid answer choices that have definitive words like "exactly," and "always."

Switchback Words

Stay alert for "switchbacks." These are the words and phrases frequently used to alert you to shifts in thought. The most common switchback word is "but." Others include "although," "however," "nevertheless," "on the other hand," "even though," "while," "in spite of," "despite," and "regardless of."

New Information

Correct answer choices will rarely have completely new information included. Answer choices typically are straightforward reflections of the material asked about and will directly relate to the question. If a new piece of information is included in an answer choice that doesn't even seem to relate to the topic being asked about, then that answer choice is likely incorrect. All of the information needed to answer the question is usually provided for you in the question. You should not have to make guesses that are unsupported or choose answer choices that require unknown information that cannot be reasoned from what is given.

Time Management

On technical questions, don't get lost on the technical terms. Don't spend too much time on any one question. If you don't know what a term means, then odds are you aren't going to get much further since you don't have a dictionary. You should be able to immediately recognize whether or not you know a term. If you don't, work with the other clues that you have—the other answer choices and terms provided— but don't waste too much time trying to figure out a difficult term that you don't know.

Contextual Clues

Look for contextual clues. An answer can be right but not the correct answer. The contextual clues will help you find the answer that is most right and is correct. Understand the context in which a phrase or statement is made. This will help you make important distinctions.

Don't Panic

Panicking will not answer any questions for you; therefore, it isn't helpful. When you first see the question, if your mind goes blank, take a deep breath. Force yourself to mechanically go through the steps of solving the problem using the strategies you've learned.

Pace Yourself

Don't get clock fever. It's easy to be overwhelmed when you're looking at a page full of questions, your mind is full of random thoughts and feeling confused, and the clock is ticking down faster than you would like. Calm down and maintain the pace that you have set for yourself. As long as you are on track by monitoring your pace, you are guaranteed to have enough time for yourself. When you get to the last few minutes of the test, it may seem like you won't have enough time left, but if you only have as many questions as you should have left at that point, then you're right on track!

Answer Selection

The best way to pick an answer choice is to eliminate all of those that are wrong, until only one is left and confirm that is the correct answer. Sometimes though, an answer choice may immediately look right. Be careful! Take a second to make sure that the other choices are not equally obvious. Don't make a hasty mistake. There are only two times that you should stop before checking other answers. First is when you are positive that the answer choice you have selected is correct. Second is when time is almost out and you have to make a quick guess!

Check Your Work

Since you will probably not know every term listed and the answer to every question, it is important that you get credit for the ones that you do know. Don't miss any questions through careless mistakes. If at all possible, try to take a second to look back over your answer selection and make sure you've selected the correct answer choice and haven't made a costly careless mistake (such as marking an answer choice that you didn't mean to mark). The time it takes for this quick double check should more than pay for itself in caught mistakes.

Beware of Directly Quoted Answers

Sometimes an answer choice will repeat word for word a portion of the question or reference section. However, beware of such exact duplication. It may be a trap! More than likely, the correct choice will paraphrase or summarize a point, rather than being exactly the same wording.

Slang

Scientific sounding answers are better than slang ones. An answer choice that begins "To compare the outcomes..." is much more likely to be correct than one that begins "Because some people insisted..."

Extreme Statements

Avoid wild answers that throw out highly controversial ideas that are proclaimed as established fact. An answer choice that states the "process should used in certain situations, if..." is much more likely to be correct than one that states the "process should be discontinued completely." The first is a calm rational statement and doesn't even make a definitive, uncompromising stance, using a hedge word "if" to provide wiggle room, whereas the second choice is a radical idea and far more extreme.

Answer Choice Families

When you have two or more answer choices that are direct opposites or parallels, one of them is usually the correct answer. For instance, if one answer choice states "x increases" and another answer choice states "x decreases" or "y increases," then those two or three answer choices are very similar in construction and fall into the same family of answer choices. A family of answer choices consists of two or three answer choices, very similar in construction, but often with directly opposite meanings. Usually the correct answer choice will be in that family of answer choices. The "odd man out" or answer choice that doesn't seem to fit the parallel construction of the other answer choices is more likely to be incorrect.

How to Overcome Test Anxiety

The very nature of tests caters to some level of anxiety, nervousness, or tension, just as we feel for any important event that occurs in our lives. A little bit of anxiety or nervousness can be a good thing. It helps us with motivation, and makes achievement just that much sweeter. However, too much anxiety can be a problem, especially if it hinders our ability to function and perform.

"Test anxiety," is the term that refers to the emotional reactions that some test-takers experience when faced with a test or exam. Having a fear of testing and exams is based upon a rational fear, since the test-taker's performance can shape the course of an academic career. Nevertheless, experiencing excessive fear of examinations will only interfere with the test-taker's ability to perform and chance to be successful.

There are a large variety of causes that can contribute to the development and sensation of test anxiety. These include, but are not limited to, lack of preparation and worrying about issues surrounding the test.

Lack of Preparation

Lack of preparation can be identified by the following behaviors or situations:

Not scheduling enough time to study, and therefore cramming the night before the test or exam
Managing time poorly, to create the sensation that there is not enough time to do everything
Failing to organize the text information in advance, so that the study material consists of the entire text and not simply the pertinent information
Poor overall studying habits

Worrying, on the other hand, can be related to both the test taker, or many other factors around him/her that will be affected by the results of the test. These include worrying about:

Previous performances on similar exams, or exams in general
How friends and other students are achieving
The negative consequences that will result from a poor grade or failure

There are three primary elements to test anxiety. Physical components, which involve the same typical bodily reactions as those to acute anxiety (to be discussed below). Emotional factors have to do with fear or panic. Mental or cognitive issues concerning attention spans and memory abilities.

Physical Signals

There are many different symptoms of test anxiety, and these are not limited to mental and emotional strain. Frequently there are a range of physical signals that will let a test taker know that he/she is suffering from test anxiety. These bodily changes can include the following:

Perspiring
Sweaty palms
Wet, trembling hands
Nausea
Dry mouth
A knot in the stomach
Headache
Faintness
Muscle tension
Aching shoulders, back and neck
Rapid heart beat
Feeling too hot/cold

To recognize the sensation of test anxiety, a test-taker should monitor him/herself for the following sensations:

The physical distress symptoms as listed above
Emotional sensitivity, expressing emotional feelings such as the need to cry or laugh too much, or a sensation of anger or helplessness
A decreased ability to think, causing the test-taker to blank out or have racing thoughts that are hard to organize or control.

Though most students will feel some level of anxiety when faced with a test or exam, the majority can cope with that anxiety and maintain it at a manageable level. However, those who cannot are faced with a very real and very serious condition, which can and should be controlled for the immeasurable benefit of this sufferer.

Naturally, these sensations lead to negative results for the testing experience. The most common effects of test anxiety have to do with nervousness and mental blocking.

Nervousness

Nervousness can appear in several different levels:

The test-taker's difficulty, or even inability to read and understand the questions on the test
The difficulty or inability to organize thoughts to a coherent form

The difficulty or inability to recall key words and concepts relating to the testing questions (especially essays)
The receipt of poor grades on a test, though the test material was well known by the test taker

Conversely, a person may also experience mental blocking, which involves:

Blanking out on test questions
Only remembering the correct answers to the questions when the test has already finished.

Fortunately for test anxiety sufferers, beating these feelings, to a large degree, has to do with proper preparation. When a test taker has a feeling of preparedness, then anxiety will be dramatically lessened.

The first step to resolving anxiety issues is to distinguish which of the two types of anxiety are being suffered. If the anxiety is a direct result of a lack of preparation, this should be considered a normal reaction, and the anxiety level (as opposed to the test results) shouldn't be anything to worry about. However, if, when adequately prepared, the test-taker still panics, blanks out, or seems to overreact, this is not a fully rational reaction. While this can be considered normal too, there are many ways to combat and overcome these effects.

Remember that anxiety cannot be entirely eliminated, however, there are ways to minimize it, to make the anxiety easier to manage. Preparation is one of the best ways to minimize test anxiety. Therefore the following techniques are wise in order to best fight off any anxiety that may want to build.

To begin with, try to avoid cramming before a test, whenever it is possible. By trying to memorize an entire term's worth of information in one day, you'll be shocking your system, and not giving yourself a very good chance to absorb the information. This is an easy path to anxiety, so for those who suffer from test anxiety, cramming should not even be considered an option.

Instead of cramming, work throughout the semester to combine all of the material which is presented throughout the semester, and work on it gradually as the course goes by, making sure to master the main concepts first, leaving minor details for a week or so before the test.

To study for the upcoming exam, be sure to pose questions that may be on the examination, to gauge the ability to answer them by integrating the ideas from your texts, notes and lectures, as well as any supplementary readings.

If it is truly impossible to cover all of the information that was covered in that particular term, concentrate on the most important portions, that can be covered very well. Learn these concepts as best as possible, so that when the test comes, a goal can be made to use these concepts as presentations of your knowledge.

In addition to study habits, changes in attitude are critical to beating a struggle with test anxiety. In fact, an improvement of the perspective over the entire test-taking experience can actually help a test taker to enjoy studying and therefore improve the overall experience. Be certain not to overemphasize the significance of the grade - know that the result of the test is neither a reflection of self worth, nor is it a measure of intelligence; one grade will not predict a person's future success.
To improve an overall testing outlook, the following steps should be tried:

Keeping in mind that the most reasonable expectation for taking a test is to expect to try to demonstrate as much of what you know as you possibly can.
Reminding ourselves that a test is only one test; this is not the only one, and there will be others.
The thought of thinking of oneself in an irrational, all-or-nothing term should be avoided at all costs.
A reward should be designated for after the test, so there's something to look forward to. Whether it be going to a movie, going out to eat, or simply visiting friends, schedule it in advance, and do it no matter what result is expected on the exam.

Test-takers should also keep in mind that the basics are some of the most important things, even beyond anti-anxiety techniques and studying. Never neglect the basic social, emotional and biological needs, in order to try to absorb information. In order to best achieve, these three factors must be held as just as important as the studying itself.

Study Steps

Remember the following important steps for studying:

Maintain healthy nutrition and exercise habits. Continue both your recreational activities and social pass times. These both contribute to your physical and emotional well being.
Be certain to get a good amount of sleep, especially the night before the test, because when you're overtired you are not able to perform to the best of your best ability.
Keep the studying pace to a moderate level by taking breaks when they are needed, and varying the work whenever possible, to keep the mind fresh instead of getting bored.
When enough studying has been done that all the material that can be learned has been learned, and the test taker is prepared for the test, stop studying and do something relaxing such as listening to music, watching a movie, or taking a warm bubble bath.

There are also many other techniques to minimize the uneasiness or apprehension that is experienced along with test anxiety before, during, or even after the examination. In fact, there are a great deal of things that can be done to stop anxiety from interfering with lifestyle and performance. Again, remember that anxiety will not be eliminated entirely, and it shouldn't be. Otherwise that "up" feeling for exams would not exist, and most of us depend on that sensation to perform better than usual. However, this anxiety has to be at a level that is manageable.

Of course, as we have just discussed, being prepared for the exam is half the battle right away. Attending all classes, finding out what knowledge will be expected on the exam, and knowing the exam schedules are easy steps to lowering anxiety. Keeping up with work will remove the need to cram, and efficient study habits will eliminate wasted time. Studying should be done in an ideal location for concentration, so that it is simple to become interested in the material and give it complete attention. A method such as SQ3R (Survey, Question, Read, Recite, Review) is a wonderful key to follow to make sure that the study habits are as effective as possible, especially in the case of learning from a textbook. Flashcards are great techniques for memorization. Learning to take good notes will mean that notes will be full of useful information, so that less sifting will need to be done to seek out what is pertinent for studying. Reviewing notes after class and then again on occasion will keep the information fresh in the mind. From notes that have been taken summary sheets and outlines can be made for simpler reviewing.

A study group can also be a very motivational and helpful place to study, as there will be a sharing of ideas, all of the minds can work together, to make sure that everyone understands, and the studying will be made more interesting because it will be a social occasion.

Basically, though, as long as the test-taker remains organized and self confident, with efficient study habits, less time will need to be spent studying, and higher grades will be achieved.

To become self confident, there are many useful steps. The first of these is "self talk." It has been shown through extensive research, that self-talk for students who suffer from test anxiety, should be well monitored, in order to make sure that it contributes to self confidence as opposed to sinking the student. Frequently the self talk of test-anxious students is negative or self-defeating, thinking that everyone else is smarter and faster, that they always mess up, and that if they don't do well, they'll fail the entire course. It is important to decreasing anxiety that awareness is made of self talk. Try writing any negative self thoughts and then disputing them with a positive statement instead. Begin self-encouragement as though it was a friend speaking. Repeat positive statements to help reprogram the mind to believing in successes instead of failures.

Helpful Techniques

Other extremely helpful techniques include:

Self-visualization of doing well and reaching goals
While aiming for an "A" level of understanding, don't try to "overprotect" by setting your expectations lower. This will only convince the mind to stop studying in order to meet the lower expectations.
Don't make comparisons with the results or habits of other students. These are individual factors, and different things work for different people, causing different results.
Strive to become an expert in learning what works well, and what can be done in order to improve. Consider collecting this data in a journal.
Create rewards for after studying instead of doing things before studying that will only turn into avoidance behaviors.
Make a practice of relaxing - by using methods such as progressive relaxation, self-hypnosis, guided imagery, etc - in order to make relaxation an automatic sensation. Work on creating a state of relaxed concentration so that concentrating will take on the focus of the mind, so that none will be wasted on worrying.
Take good care of the physical self by eating well and getting enough sleep.
Plan in time for exercise and stick to this plan.

Beyond these techniques, there are other methods to be used before, during and after the test that will help the test-taker perform well in addition to overcoming anxiety.

Before the exam comes the academic preparation. This involves establishing a study schedule and beginning at least one week before the actual date of the test. By doing this, the anxiety of not having enough time to study for the test will be automatically eliminated. Moreover, this will make the studying a much more effective experience, ensuring that the learning will be an easier process. This relieves much undue pressure on the test-taker.

Summary sheets, note cards, and flash cards with the main concepts and examples of these main concepts should be prepared in advance of the actual studying time. A topic should never be eliminated from this process. By omitting a topic because it isn't expected to be on the test is only setting up the test-taker for anxiety should it actually appear on the exam. Utilize the course syllabus for laying out the topics that should be studied. Carefully go over the notes that were made in class, paying special attention to any of the issues that the professor took special care to emphasize while lecturing in class. In the textbooks, use the chapter review, or if possible, the chapter tests, to begin your review.

It may even be possible to ask the instructor what information will be covered on the exam, or what the format of the exam will be (for example, multiple choice, essay, free form, true-false). Additionally, see if it is possible to find out how many questions will be on the test. If a review sheet or sample test has been offered by the professor, make good use of it, above anything else, for the preparation for the test. Another great resource for getting to know the examination is reviewing tests from previous semesters. Use these tests to review, and aim to achieve a 100% score on each of the possible topics. With a few exceptions, the goal that you set for yourself is the highest one that you will reach.

Take all of the questions that were assigned as homework, and rework them to any other possible course material. The more problems reworked, the more skill and confidence will form as a result. When forming the solution to a problem, write out each of the steps. Don't simply do head work. By doing as many steps on paper as possible, much clarification and therefore confidence will be formed. Do this with as many homework problems as possible, before checking the answers. By checking the answer after each problem, a reinforcement will exist, that will not be on the exam. Study situations should be as exam-like as possible, to prime the test-taker's system for the experience. By waiting to check the answers at the end, a psychological advantage will be formed, to decrease the stress factor.

Another fantastic reason for not cramming is the avoidance of confusion in concepts, especially when it comes to mathematics. 8-10 hours of study will become one hundred percent more effective if it is spread out over a week or at least several days, instead of doing it all in one sitting. Recognize that the human brain requires time in order to assimilate new material, so frequent breaks and a span of study time over several days will be much more beneficial.

Additionally, don't study right up until the point of the exam. Studying should stop a minimum of one hour before the exam begins. This allows the brain to rest and put things in their proper order. This will also provide the time to become as relaxed as possible when going into the examination room. The test-taker will also have time to eat well and eat sensibly. Know that the brain needs food as much as the rest of the body. With enough food and enough sleep, as well as a relaxed attitude, the body and the mind are primed for success.

Avoid any anxious classmates who are talking about the exam. These students only spread anxiety, and are not worth sharing the anxious sentimentalities.

Before the test also involves creating a positive attitude, so mental preparation should also be a point of concentration. There are many keys to creating a positive attitude. Should fears become rushing in, make a visualization of taking the exam, doing well, and seeing an A written on the paper. Write out a list of affirmations that will bring a feeling of confidence, such as "I am doing well in my English class," "I studied well and know my material," "I enjoy this class." Even if the affirmations aren't believed at first, it sends a positive message to the subconscious which will result in an alteration of the overall belief system, which is the system that creates reality.

If a sensation of panic begins, work with the fear and imagine the very worst! Work through the entire scenario of not passing the test, failing the entire course, and dropping out of school, followed by not getting a job, and pushing a shopping cart through the dark alley where you'll live. This will place things into perspective! Then, practice deep breathing and create a visualization of the opposite situation - achieving an "A" on the exam, passing the entire course, receiving the degree at a graduation ceremony.

On the day of the test, there are many things to be done to ensure the best results, as well as the most calm outlook. The following stages are suggested in order to maximize test-taking potential:

Begin the examination day with a moderate breakfast, and avoid any coffee or beverages with caffeine if the test taker is prone to jitters. Even people who are used to managing caffeine can feel jittery or light-headed when it is taken on a test day.

Attempt to do something that is relaxing before the examination begins. As last minute cramming clouds the mastering of overall concepts, it is better to use this time to create a calming outlook.

Be certain to arrive at the test location well in advance, in order to provide time to select a location that is away from doors, windows and other distractions, as well as giving enough time to relax before the test begins.

Keep away from anxiety generating classmates who will upset the sensation of stability and relaxation that is being attempted before the exam.

Should the waiting period before the exam begins cause anxiety, create a self-distraction by reading a light magazine or something else that is relaxing and simple.

During the exam itself, read the entire exam from beginning to end, and find out how much time should be allotted to each individual problem. Once writing the exam, should more time be taken for a problem, it should be abandoned, in order to begin another problem. If there is time at the end, the unfinished problem can always be returned to and completed.

Read the instructions very carefully - twice - so that unpleasant surprises won't follow during or after the exam has ended.

When writing the exam, pretend that the situation is actually simply the completion of homework within a library, or at home. This will assist in forming a relaxed atmosphere, and will allow the brain extra focus for the complex thinking function.

Begin the exam with all of the questions with which the most confidence is felt. This will build the confidence level regarding the entire exam and will begin a quality momentum. This will also create encouragement for trying the problems where uncertainty resides.

Going with the "gut instinct" is always the way to go when solving a problem. Second guessing should be avoided at all costs. Have confidence in the ability to do well.

For essay questions, create an outline in advance that will keep the mind organized and make certain that all of the points are remembered. For multiple choice, read every answer, even if the correct one has been spotted - a better one may exist.

Continue at a pace that is reasonable and not rushed, in order to be able to work carefully. Provide enough time to go over the answers at the end, to check for small errors that can be corrected.

Should a feeling of panic begin, breathe deeply, and think of the feeling of the body releasing sand through its pores. Visualize a calm, peaceful place, and include all of the sights, sounds and sensations of this image. Continue the deep breathing, and take a few minutes to continue this with closed eyes. When all is well again, return to the test.

If a "blanking" occurs for a certain question, skip it and move on to the next question. There will be time to return to the other question later. Get everything done that can be done, first, to guarantee all the grades that can be compiled, and to build all of the confidence possible. Then return to the weaker questions to build the marks from there.

Remember, one's own reality can be created, so as long as the belief is there, success will follow. And remember: anxiety can happen later, right now, there's an exam to be written!

After the examination is complete, whether there is a feeling for a good grade or a bad grade, don't dwell on the exam, and be certain to follow through on the reward that was promised...and enjoy it! Don't dwell on any mistakes that have been made, as there is nothing that can be done at this point anyway.

Additionally, don't begin to study for the next test right away. Do something relaxing for a while, and let the mind relax and prepare itself to begin absorbing information again.

From the results of the exam - both the grade and the entire experience, be certain to learn from what has gone on. Perfect studying habits and work some more on confidence in order to make the next examination experience even better than the last one.

Learn to avoid places where openings occurred for laziness, procrastination and day dreaming.

Use the time between this exam and the next one to better learn to relax, even learning to relax on cue, so that any anxiety can be controlled during the next exam. Learn how to relax the body. Slouch in your chair if that helps. Tighten and then relax all of the different muscle groups, one group at a time, beginning with the feet and then working all the way up to the neck and face. This will ultimately relax the muscles more than they were to begin with. Learn how to breathe deeply and comfortably, and focus on this breathing going in and out as a relaxing thought. With every exhale, repeat the word "relax."

As common as test anxiety is, it is very possible to overcome it. Make yourself one of the test-takers who overcome this frustrating hindrance.

Additional Bonus Material

Due to our efforts to try to keep this book to a manageable length, we've created a link that will give you access to all of your additional bonus material.

Please visit http://www.mometrix.com/bonus948/reghsenglacc to access the information.